JAMES
FENIMORE COOPER

J. Fenemore Cooper

JAMES
FENIMORE COOPER

BY

MARY E. PHILLIPS

NEW YORK: JOHN LANE COMPANY
LONDON: JOHN LANE: THE BODLEY HEAD
TORONTO: BELL AND COCKBURN
MCMXIII

6
.C7862P

THE UNIVERSITY PRESS, CAMBRIDGE, U. S. A.

178464

DEDICATED TO THE YOUNG OF
ALL AGES FROM THE YEARS OF TEN
TO TEN TIMES TEN

PREFACE

The intention of this simply told *personal* life of James Fenimore Cooper, the creator of American romance, is to have all material *authentic*. The pictures of men, women, places and things are, as nearly as possible, of Cooper's association with them to reproduce a background of his time and to make the *man* — not the author — its central foreground figure. From every available source since the earliest mention of the author's name, both in print and out, material for these pages has been collected. In this wide gleaning in the field of letters — a rich harvest from able and brilliant pens — the gleaner hereby expresses grateful appreciation of these transplanted values. Much, precious in worth and attractive in interest, comes into these pages from the generous and good among the relatives, friends, and admirers of Fenimore Cooper. And more than all others, the author's grand-nephew, the late Mr. George Pomeroy Keese, of Cooperstown, New York, has paid rich and rare tribute to the memory of his uncle, with whom when a boy he came in living touch. Appeals to Cooper's grandson, James Fenimore Cooper, Esq., of Albany, New York, and also to his publishers have been met in a spirit so gracious and their giving has been so generous as to command the grateful service of the writer.

For rare values, in service and material, special credits are due to Mr. George Pomeroy Keese, Cooperstown, N. Y.; James Fenimore Cooper, Esq., Albany, N. Y.; Mr. Francis Whiting Halsey, New York City; Mr. Edwin Tenney Stiger, Watertown, Mass.; General James Grant Wilson, New York City; Mr. Horace G. Wadlin, Librarian, Messrs. Otto Fleischner, Assistant Librarian, O. A. Bierstadt, F. C. Blaisdell, and others, of the Boston Public Library; Miss Alice Bailey Keese, Cooperstown, N. Y.; Mrs. T. Henry Dewey, Paris, France; Mrs. Edward Emerson Waters, New York City; and Miss Mary C. Sheridan, Boston, Mass.

MARY E. PHILLIPS.

INTRODUCTION

A LIFE of Cooper, written with some particular reference to the picturesque village among the Otsego hills, where he so long lived and in whose soil he, for some sixty years or more, has slept, has long been needed. That such a book should have become a labor of love in the hands of Miss Phillips is not more interesting than it is fortunate that the task should have been accomplished so conspicuously well. Miss Phillips has borne testimony to the resourcefulness and rare devotion with which the late Mr. Keese assisted her in researches extending over many years. None knew so well as he the personal side of Cooper's whole life story; none so assiduously and so lovingly, during a long life spent in Cooperstown, gathered and tried to preserve in their integrity every significant and interesting detail of it.

The turning point in Cooper's life was reached when he went to Cooperstown, although he was little more than a child in arms. Most curious is it that his going should have resulted from the foreclosure of a mortgage. This mortgage had been given in the late Colonial period by George Croghan, and covered a vast tract of native forest lands in Otsego. In these lands, through the foreclosure, Cooper's father, soon after the Revolution, acquired a large interest, which led him to abandon his home of ease and refinement in Burlington, New Jersey, and found a new, and, as it proved to be, a permanent one in the unpeopled wilderness at the foot of Otsego Lake. Except for this accident of fortune, Leatherstocking and his companions of the forest never could have been created by the pen of Cooper.

Francis W. Halsey.

ILLUSTRATIONS

[xiii]

[xiv]

[xvi]

[xvii]

[xix]

[xx]

[xxi]

Acknowledgment is due The F. A. Ringler
Company of New York City and Messrs. John
Andrew and Son of Boston, Mass., for the care
and interest they have shown in making the cuts
used in this volume.

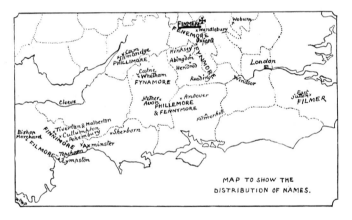

MAP TO SHOW THE
DISTRIBUTION OF NAMES.

The English Fynamore Country and Family Arms.

[xxiv]

JAMES FENIMORE COOPER

COOPER'S BIRTHPLACE, BURLINGTON, N. J.

T HE light of this world fell on James Fenimore
Cooper September 15, 1789. The founder of
American romance was born in a quaint, two-
storied house of stuccoed brick which now num-
bers 457 Main St., Burlington, New Jersey. It
was then " the last house but one as you go into
the country " and among the best of the town.
In a like house next door lived the father of the
naval hero, Capt. James Lawrence. These two
houses opened directly on the street and their
slanting roofs were shaded by tall trees rooted
at the curbstones. This outline of Fenimore

[1]

Cooper's birthplace is from the text-picture in " Literary Rambles," by Theodore F. Wolfe, M.D., Ph.D. The first of his father's family in this new country was James Cooper, who came from Stratford-on-Avon, England, in 1679. He and his wife were Quakers, and with Quaker thrift bought wide tracts of land in New Jersey and Pennsylvania. Seventy-five years after James Cooper stepped on American soil his great-grandson William was born, December 2, 1754, in Byberry township, Pennsylvania.

On December 12, 1775, at Burlington, New Jersey, William Cooper married Elizabeth, daughter of Richard Fenimore, whose family came from Oxfordshire of Old England, and, at intervals, held office in her provinces. James, the future author and named for his grandfather Cooper, was the eleventh of twelve children. About 1807 Cooper, by request of his mother, said he would adopt the name of Fenimore as there were no men of her family to continue it. The change was delayed by the untimely death of Judge Cooper, and also to make less difficult the settlement of his large estate. But in 1826 James Cooper applied to the legislature for his change of name to

James Cooper *Fenimore*. This request was not granted, but the change to "James Fenimore Cooper" was made. Cooper's comment on this outcome is a graphic record and "suggests," says an authority, that "the legislature would do well to assume that a petitioner,

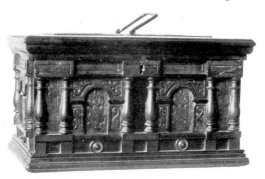

THE FENIMORE BOX.

in such a case, knew better than they did what he wanted." The hyphen, at first used, was soon dropped. And so it was for his mother's sake that he made world-wide his fame by the name of James *Fenimore* Cooper.

"The Fenimore Box" is an "English measure box, curious, and centuries old, brought over by the first of the name." It descended to Cooper from his mother, Elizabeth Fenimore, and is now treasured as a family heirloom by his grandson, James Fenimore Cooper of Albany, New York.

As the first James Cooper and his wife were Quakers, perchance the same Quaker thrift in-

THE SUSQUEHANNA.

fluenced William Cooper to follow the lead of George Washington, who, two years before, in order to find out the inland waterways of our country, came from the Mohawk Valley to the headwaters of the Susquehanna — this stream which Fenimore Cooper called " the crooked river to which the Atlantic herself extended an arm of welcome." Lake Otsego — the " Glimmerglass " — William Cooper saw first in the autumn of 1785. " Mt. Vision " was covered with a forest growth so dense that he had to

[4]

" climb a tree in order to get a view of the lake, and while up the tree " he saw a deer come down " from the thickets and quietly drink of its waters near Otsego Rock." " Just where the

CHINGACHGOOK ON COUNCIL ROCK.

Susquehanna leaves the Lake on its long journey to the sea " this famous Council Rock " still shows its chin above the water and marks the spot where Deerslayer met Chingachgook the Great Serpent of the Delawares." Now " its lake margin belongs to a grandson of the author, who also bears his name," is a record found in Dr. Wolfe's " Literary Haunts and Homes." In the red man's tongue Otsego means " a place of friendly meeting " of Indian warriors. The author of " Deerslayer " has immortalized that lake-country in the opening chapter of this book. Of this visit to his future home and lands William Cooper has written: " In 1785 I visited the rough and hilly country of Otsego. I was alone, three hundred miles from home, without food of any kind. I caught trout in the brook and roasted them in the ashes. My horse fed on the grass that grew by the edge of the waters. I laid me down to sleep in my watch-coat, nothing but the wilderness about me. In this way I explored the country and formed my plans of future settlement. May, 1786, I opened a sale of forty thousand acres of land, which in sixteen days were all taken up by the poorest order of men." Here William Cooper laid out

COUNCIL ROCK.

the site of Cooperstown, which, until 1791, when it became the county-town, was at times also called "Foot-of-the-Lake." He built a store for his sturdy pioneers, giving credit for their simple needs of life, and traded settlement products for them. His tenants put up log houses, and paid rent in butter, wheat, corn, oats, maple-sugar, and finally in pork; — so much that rentals known as "pork leases" were sold like farms. Money was scarce in those days, — when one John Miller, and his father, coming to the Lakeland's point of the river, felled a pine, over which they crossed to the Cooperstown site. Its stump was marked with white paint and called the "bridge-tree" by Fenimore Cooper. His sister Nancy's grandson, Mr. George Pomeroy Keese, from whom much will appear in these pages, has all there is left of that stump.

In a few years the town's growth gave such promise that William Cooper began to build his own home. It was generally known as "The Manor," but the patent of Cooperstown was not according to law a manor. It was finished in 1788, when a few streets were laid out and the town's first map was made. And October 10, 1790,

[7]

he brought his family and servants, some fifteen persons, and their belongings, from Burlington, New Jersey, to this early pioneer home. Mr. Keese says that " The Manor " was of wood with outside boarding, unplaned; that it was two stories high, had two wings and a back building added in 1791. It first stood facing Main St. and Otsego Lake and directly in front of the later Otsego Hall, now marked by the Indian Hunter. In 1799 it was moved down the street, and was burned down in 1812. In its time it was the most stately private house for miles around. The second home, Otsego Hall, built in 1798, was of bricks which were made at the outlet of the lake. It had seventy feet of frontage by fifty-six of depth, and had two stories with attic and basement. The main hall measured twenty-four by forty-eight feet and the rooms on either side were twenty feet wide. Otsego Hall is said to have been of the exact, generous proportions of the Van Rensselaer Manor House at Albany, New York, where Judge Cooper was a frequent visitor. His own Hall home on Otsego's southern shore ever had " the air and capacity of a mansion and a history of hospitality well deserved."

THE MANOR HOUSE.

THE ORIGINAL OTSEGO HALL.

William Cooper
of Coopers Town

To a friend William Cooper wrote: "I began life with a small capital and a large family, and yet I have already settled more acres than any man in America; and I trust no one can justly impute to me any act of oppression. Your good sense and knowledge will excuse this seeming boast." He elsewhere said that he owed his success to "a steady mind, a sober judgment, fortitude, perseverance, and above all, common sense." And here he lived as a wise and kind landlord among his people. For nine years he was First Judge of the County Court of Common Pleas, and he served two terms in Congress. Of Judge William Cooper there are three portraits, — Gilbert Stuart's of 1797–98, Trumbull's of 1806, and one by an unknown artist. His kindly gray eye, robust figure, and firm expression bear out the story of his life as told by these portraits.

James Fenimore Cooper, in a letter to his wife, dated Canajoharie, 1834, wrote of his father: "I have been up to the ravine to the old Frey house. It recalled my noble-looking, warm-hearted, witty father, with his deep laugh, sweet voice, and fine, rich eye, as he used to light the way with his anecdotes and fun. Old Frey, with his little black peepers, pipe, hearty laugh, broken English, and warm welcome, was in the background. I went to the very spot where one of the old man's slaves amused Sam and myself with an imitation of a turkey that no artist has ever yet been able to supplant in my memory." This Heindrick Frey was a noted character of the Mohawk Valley over one hundred years ago.

It was, however, to the first home on Otsego's shore that the future creator of American romance was brought when a babe some thirteen months old. Here, in the heart of the wilderness, his infancy was passed. Otsego Hall sheltered his budding boyhood and young manhood. Grace and refinement dwelt within the household; without, voices of the forest awakened and nurtured his naturally active mind, which later on was not less influenced by the mysteries of the sea. The Six Nations were yet a power in the Mohawk Valley, then the highway to the land of the setting sun beyond. And they are now remembered in the names of the principal lakes and streams of the country that once was theirs. The boy was face-to-face with the " grim warriors, braves, and chieftains that the man, Fenimore Cooper, translated into his pages, with a touch true to the red man's life," his instinct in trading, his friendly and hostile intent. Here Nature was his first and unforgettable teacher. From "Pages and Pictures," by his daughter, Susan Fenimore Cooper, much will be given in this book. Miss Cooper has drawn some pretty pen-pictures of her father's child-life. She writes: "From the first bow and arrow, kite and ball, to later feats in fishing, riding, shooting, and skating, all were connected with his highland home." He was "healthy and active; a brave, blithe-hearted, impetuous, most generous and upright boy." Of his childhood another record is: "A gray-eyed, light-haired, ruddy boy, nimble as a deer and gay as a bird; on the lake, plying his oar lustily or trimming his sail to the mountain breeze; and whenever he found a wave high enough to lift his little boat, his veins would thrill with a strange delight, and he would ask himself whether this was like those ocean waves of which he had heard such wonders." The little lad's next step in learning was taken under the gentle rule of his elder sister, Hannah, who had her schooling in New York City, and afterwards improved her leisure by extensive reading. She was a model of domestic virtues and was greatly beloved, especially by the poor, to whom she was

Willm Henry Harrison

ever an angel of mercy. She often went with her father on his official visits to the seat of government, and when, in 1800, at the age of twenty-three years, she lost her life by a fall from her horse, her early death was widely and deeply mourned. Her memory was always cherished with peculiar tenderness by her brother James, the special charge of her loving care.

A letter, written by him in 1841 to his old "messmate," Commodore Shubrick, reveals no wane of Cooper's love for and pride in this sister, and his letter's " political discovery " reveals that

WILLIAM HENRY HARRISON, 1800.

Miss Cooper's attractions were as fully appreciated by the eminent of her own country as by those of foreign shores. So comes into these pages a youthful, slender romance of the later hero of Tippecanoe and still later President of the United States.

OTSEGO HALL, COOPERSTOWN,
February, 28, 1841.

I have made a great political discovery lately, which must not go any further than Mrs. Shubrick and Mary. In 1799, when Congress sat in Philadelphia, my father was a member, as was also General Harrison. You know I had a sister killed by a fall from a horse in

[15]

1800. This sister passed the Winter in Philadelphia with my father. Miss Anne Cooper [the author's daughter] was lately in Philadelphia, where she met Mr. Thomas Biddle, who asked if our family were not Harrison men. The reason of so singular a question was asked, and Mr. Biddle answered that in 1799 Mr. Harrison was dying with love for Miss Cooper, that he (Mr. Biddle) was his confidant, and that he *thinks* but does not *know* that he was refused. If not refused it was because he was not encouraged to propose, so you see I stand on high grounds and am ready to serve you on occasion. Don't let this go any further, however. I confess to think all the better of the General for this discovery, for it shows that he had forty years ago both taste and judgment in a matter in which men so often fail. Mary will open her eyes at this somewhat wider than ever, but she must not open her mouth until she gives her allegiance to him who will know all her thoughts. With best regards

Yours as ever,

J. FENIMORE COOPER.

NOTE. — Later light on the subject reveals Mr. Harrison's " dying of love " as a hearty admiration and esteem for the rare grace and charm of character, mind, and person possessed by Judge Cooper's young daughter.

During 1795 many distinguished exiles came to this new-country home, and among those who found their way to Otsego Hall was the Marquis de Talleyrand, who was pleased to write an

TALLEYRAND.

acrostic on Miss Cooper, then seventeen. The
famous Frenchman's record, in part, of this visit
was "*Otsego n'est pas gai.*" Compared to the
France of Talleyrand's day this record was
true. The *Otsego Herald's* motto of that time
was

Historic truth our *Herald* shall proclaim,
The Law our guide, the public good our aim.

[17]

In its issue of October 2, 1795, appeared the celebrated diplomat's Acrostic.

Aimable philosophe au printemps de son âge,
Ni les temps, ni les lieus n'altèrent son esprit ;
Ne cèdent qu' à ses goûts simples et son étalage,
Au milieu des deserts, elle lit, pense, écrit.

Cultivez, belle Anna, votre goût pour l'étude ;
On ne saurait ici mieux employer son temps ;
Otsego n'est pas gai — mais, tout est habitude ;
Paris vous déplairait fort au premier moment ;
Et qui jouit de soi dans une solitude,
Rentrant au monde, est sur d'en faire l'ornement.

In affectionate remembrance of Miss Cooper the hill just northwest of Cooperstown was named for her, and " Hannah's Hill " commands one of the town's finest views. In the quiet shades of Christ's Church yard " belle Anna " rests beneath a slab bearing some lines by her father, but not her name.

The August before this sad event Judge Cooper gave the first of the many " lake parties " that floated over Otsego — " which no waters can rival." In the fairness of her youth Miss Hannah was there with her little sister, later Mrs. Pomeroy ; and also, among the gay " five and twenty friends from Philadelphia," were their brothers. Indian canoes and flat-bottomed skiffs conveyed them to the eastern shore, where, at Two-Mile Point, a frightened fawn, startled from its forest home by the dogs of Shipman the hunter, — who later outlined " Leatherstocking," — darted from the leafy thicket and plunged into the lake. At once all were in motion to rescue the little creature now swimming for life. It was successfully brought to land and became a great pet with Judge Cooper's children; but one day, frightened by strange, fierce dogs, it bounded into the forest depths for refuge, and never returned.

The centennial anniversary of this first picnic was celebrated by the third and fourth generation of Judge Cooper's descendants, who met at Point Judith to honor the occasion. Of the verses written by Mr. George Pomeroy Keese concerning this event two are:

> And one hundred years have come and gone
>   Since our country then was new,
> And now we keep in memory dear
>   Our love for the good and true.

POINT JUDITH.

To one who came to his forest home
    And gave to our village its name;
To the son, the touch of whose magic pen
    Has lifted to world-wide fame.

In this summer of 1800 Richard, Judge
Cooper's eldest son, built his house of frame
on "Apple Hill." It was the second villa-like
home in the village. Its site, now known as
"Fernleigh," is the country-seat of Stephen
Clark, Esq. "Edgewater," overlooking Lake
Otsego, is the land that, after Judge Cooper's
death in 1809, fell to his son Isaac. Here, the
following year, Isaac Cooper built his home
of brick. Later, it changed in form, use, and

" Edgewater."

ownership, but again became a family possession
through the marriage of Mr. Theodore Keese
with the daughter of George Pomeroy and Ann
Cooper. Renewing in all ways the charm and
grace of its early days, " Edgewater," as the
home of Mr. George Pomeroy Keese, the grandson of Fenimore Cooper's youngest sister Ann,
commands at the foot of the lake its length,
breadth, beauty, and inspiration.

The old stone house, known as the " Deacon
Pomeroy's place," that stood at the corner of
Main and River streets, gives — in a quaint gable
— an enduring record of romance in this sister

MR. AND MRS. GEORGE POMEROY.

Ann's young life. It was built of stone in the
peculiar herring-bone style by Judge William
Cooper for a wedding gift to his only living
daughter, Ann, when she married George Pomeroy, grandson of Gen. Seth Pomeroy and lineal
descendant of that Sir Ralph de Pomeroy who
came to England with William the Conqueror.
In this quaint gable appear the intertwined letters
G. A. P. C., — the initials of the bridegroom and
bride, — with the date 1804 beneath.

The Cooper room of this old stone house,
now the home of Mrs. Benedict, a granddaughter,
shelters family portraits from William Cooper's
time down to the present day — five generations.
What stories might it not tell of the attractive
originals? Many were the letters that Fenimore

Cooper wrote from Europe to this sister, Mrs. George Pomeroy, of the old stone house.

Mrs. Benedict has also placed there many souvenirs of her sister, Constance Fenimore Woolson, gathered during her long residence in Europe, including the author's writing-table and her chair.

"Master Oliver Cory kept the village school" in those child-days of Fenimore Cooper, and long after. "He was well qualified for that post; laborious, upright, firm, yet patient and

THE OLD STONE HOUSE.

[23]

kindly by nature. His training of the boys was
excellent. Saturdays were given to religious
lessons, and he paid careful but quiet attention
to their morals and manners." From his sister
Hannah's teaching Judge Cooper's youngest son
went to Master Cory's school. It was kept in
"one of those tasteless buildings that afflict all
new countries," and here was called the "Academy." It served Cooperstown in timely ways
for religious and political meetings; public courts
were held here, and a ball was given now and
then under its roof. As to the school, time and
incident brought out a taste for music in the
pupils of Master Cory. It seems that Judge
Cooper had brought from Philadelphia a large
upright organ of imposing appearance and
power, which he placed in his manor-house hall.
Its arrival in the village made a summer's sensation. When put up and adjusted, a rehearsal
of country dances, reels, and more serious music
came floating through the broad door and ample
windows of Otsego Hall into Master Cory's
domain, the Academy, which stood in the adjoining street. As, with magic effect the strains
of "Hail Columbia" poured into the school-
room, Master Cory skilfully met a moment of

COOPERSTOWN PRIOR TO 1835.

The building on the extreme right is the Academy.

open rebellion with these words: "Boys, that organ is a remarkable instrument. You never heard the like of it before. I give you half an hour's intermission. Go into the street and listen to the music!"

These "Academy boys" were ambitious; each annual exhibition was crowded, to listen to the speeches "of Coriolanus, Iago, Brutus, and Cassius" by "raw lads from the village and adjoining farms," in all the bravery of local militia uniform — blue coats "faced with red, matross swords, and hats of '76." On such an occasion James Cooper, then a child of eight years, became the pride and admiration of Master Cory for his moving recitation of the "Beggar's Petition" — acting the part of an old man wrapped in a faded cloak and leaning over his staff. It is recorded that James had the fine, healthy pie-appetite usual to his age, for, says the record, when his eldest brother "was showing the sights of New York to the youngest, he took him to a pasty-shop, and, after watching the boy eat pasty after pasty, said to him: 'Jim, eat all you want, but remember that each one costs the old man a lot.'" Pasty then outbalanced property for "Jim."

In due time the lad outgrew the Academy's instruction, but from boy to man he never outgrew Master Cory's affection, nor his own for the dear home scenes on the shores of the "Haunted Lake," which he was so soon to leave for his first important schooling. The books he wrote later tell how he never forgot the howl of the wolf across the icy field of Otsego on cold winter nights, the peculiar wail of the sharp-toothed panther in the quiet wood roads, nor the familiar springs where the deer lingered latest. One autumn day, while still a pupil under Master Cory's charge, the future author of "The Pioneers" was at play in his father's garden, when suddenly he was surprised by a deer which came leaping over the fence from the street, almost brushing his face as it bounded away into the pine woods at the back of the house. This incident he often related to his children.

It was not long before this youngest son was sent from home. The eventful journey to Albany was made in the care of a near and worthy farmer, "who was carrying toward the Hudson a load of wheat from the fields of Otsego." They went over the fine turnpike, — the great highway of that day, — "just finished from the Hudson to Cherry Valley." The child had heard much of this wonder of roads from the gentlemen at his father's table who were interested in it, and he was eager to see its toll-gates and stone bridges. After leaving " the corduroy tracks " leading to it from Cooperstown, the famous turnpike burst upon the gratified schoolboy's vision. As they trotted slowly along the farmer pointed out, among other marvels of the way, " a tavern for every mile " of the sixty between Albany and Lake Otsego. A long train of farmers' wagons, filled with the precious wheat, was slowly rolling eastward, passing emigrant wagons of " growing families " and household gear moving westward to the great lake countries. All this delighted the boy of nine, who was finally set down at the door of St. Peter's Rectory at Albany, New York. Here for four years he became one of the four young pupils of the Rev. Thomas Ellison, rector of the church. Dr. Ellison was an Englishman and a graduate of Oxford — a rare scholar and a king's man. From him came Cooper's strong preference for English church government and equally strong feeling against the Puritans of Old and New England. While the Puritan's character was not pleasing to Cooper, he himself was called a " Puritan of Puritans," and it was to them he referred in the following: " Whatever else I may think of the Yankees, —

DR. THOMAS ELLISON.

a calmer, firmer, braver people do not walk this earth." Of this sentiment " The Wept of Wishton-Wish," published in 1829, gives ample proof.

The Rev. Joseph Hooper, author of the " History of St. Peter's Church, Albany, N. Y.," related an incident of Cooper's old Rectory school days there. The story came to Dr. Hooper from Mr. Edward Floyd de Lancy, son of Bishop de Lancy of Western New York, and is as follows:

[29]

It was the custom of the Rev. Thomas Ellison
when he became too feeble to personally direct
his workmen, to sit upon the stoop of the Rectory and watch the removal of the sandbank

St. Peter's Church, Albany, N. Y.

which covered the chosen site for the new church,
corner of State and Lodge streets.   Hundreds
of loads had to be carted away before the foun-
dation could be laid, and some of the carter's
pay tickets on quartered playing-cards are pre-
served in St. Peter's archives.   But the great
hole in the ground had a great attraction for the
boys of Albany, and they would leap into it to
play tag and leap-frog until the stern voice of
the Dominie called them to order, when they

would scamper away or hide in some corner out
of sight of the piercing eyes of Dr. Ellison.
Sometimes they would answer him mockingly,
to his great annoyance. He could not pursue

STATE STREET, ALBANY, N. Y., 1802.

them, but he could, when his own pupils joined
with the other boys, as they often did, give them
stern and severe lectures upon their conduct, for
they were playing on ground to be used for a
sacred purpose. Even the rod of correction was
used without curing them of this habit. Young
Cooper was often a ringleader, and their pranks
would often continue until darkness concealed
them from the watchful and angry Rector, to
whom, nevertheless, they gave due honor and
respect.

From one of his " Sketches of England," written
to William, Judge John Jay's second son, comes, in
part, Cooper's graphic description of Dr. Ellison:
" Thirty-six years ago you and I were school fellows and classmates in the home of a clergyman of
the true English school. This man entertained a
most profound reverence for the King and the
nobility; was not backward in expressing his con-
tempt for all classes of dissenters and all ungentle-
manly sects; was particularly severe on the im-
moralities of the French Revolution, and, though
eating our bread, was not especially lenient to our
own; compelled you and me to begin Virgil with
the eclogues, and Cicero with the knotty phrases
that open the oration in favor of the poet Archias,
because these writers would not have placed them
first in the books if they did not intend people to
read them first; spent his money freely and sometimes that of other people; was particularly te-
nacious of the ritual and of all decencies of the
Church; detested a democrat as he did the devil;
cracked his jokes daily about Mr. Jefferson, never
failing to place his libertinism in strong relief
against the approved morals of George III., of
several passages in whose history it is charitable
to suppose he was ignorant; prayed fervently on

Sunday; decried all morals, institutions, churches, manners but those of England from Monday to Saturday."

The lad from Otsego soon became a prime favorite with his tutor, who took pleasure in teaching him. The old-fashioned, heroic romances were a rare delight to him, — a taste which was thought to come from his mother, who was very fond of such reading. One vacation, at about the age of eleven, he and a playmate lost themselves in the exciting interest of such a tale; " Don Belianus of Greece " made so deep an impression on Cooper that after reading it he said seriously to his playfellow that he would write a book himself, and would " begin it at once." And, like " Don Belianus of Greece," this story was to have " knights, and squires, and horses, and ladies, and castles and banners." With the glory of his story in mind, the boy had utterly forgotten his hearty dislike of pen-work at school. But his active brain soon put to flight this hobgoblin; he thought of the bit of a blue newspaper — the *Otsego Herald* — printed in Cooperstown by the father of his comrade. So they planned to use the resting-time of the press for the printing of this new book, of which, however, only a few chapters were put in type. The new author soon wearied of his work; but none the less it was the first step in his future literary career.

During 1801 a man near fifty, cleanly clad in sailor's gear but without stockings or neck-cloth, appeared before Judge Cooper and asked if the lot between Fenimore and the village was for sale. The answer was, "Yes, but the price is high," and naming it, the stranger requested that a deed be made out at once; he counted down the amount in gold, and gave his name as Esaias Hausman. He had built for himself a small rude house on this lot and lived alone in it for years. The secrets of his former life, his wide learning (once found teaching a college president Hebrew), and disappearance at times, were never solved. Only his death revealed a purse of gold worn between his shoulder-blades. There was no will, so to public sale went the little hut and its lake-shore lot. This man of mystery made a deep impression on Cooper's boy-mind, and later, in 1838, was the subject of several pages of the author's "Chronicles of Cooperstown." Then there was James Allen, — a Scotch master-mason, — who came his way from the "Land o' Cakes" in 1801, and found, as an employee of Judge Cooper, an opening for his trade, and soon became a great favorite with the Cooper boys. This master-mason took great pride in exact work, with which no trifling was permitted. No stone could be moved but his true eye would detect it in a flash, and wild was the fury with which his fiery trowel flew for the culprit, and with such convincing force that it was wise to avoid further meddling with the "gude mon's" work. Of "Jamie Allen," master-mason and staunch *auld kirke mon*, many an amusing story is told in Fenimore Cooper's "Wyandotté, or the Hutted Knoll," written in 1843. These men among others marked the unusual in Cooper's vacations from Dr. Ellison's school-rule at Albany. Later in life he wrote a lively memory-sketch of his tutor, the rector of St. Peter's Church. But the death in 1802 of this accomplished gentleman sent his pupil — then a stripling of thirteen — to Yale. He entered the freshman 1802-3 January-term class, and, "excepting the poet Hillhouse, two weeks his junior, James Cooper was the youngest student in college." There "his progress in his studies is said to have been honorable to his talents." And " in the ancient languages he had no superior in his class."

Cooper owned to having learned little at college. When left to his own bent, his early love

" Near Shores " of New Haven.

for out-of-door life drew him to roam the hills and explore near shores, and to his first view of the grand old ocean, which later claimed his tribute of service. For a boyish frolic in his junior year the lad left Yale, and this incident ended his college career. It is of record that Judge Cooper took the boy's part against the faculty version and brought his son home. Yet something from his books James Cooper must have gleaned, for there is a story of a young sailor who, in some public place in the streets of an English port, attracted the curiosity of the

YALE COLLEGE, 1806.

crowd by explaining to his companions the meaning of a Latin motto.

The Albany, school-boy days of William Jay and James Cooper were renewed at Yale where was welded their strong life-friendship. On the college roll of their time appear amongst other names that of John C. Calhoun of South Carolina, and the scholarly poet Hillhouse of New Haven. In the Dodd, Mead & Company's 1892 issue of " William Jay and the Constitutional Movement for the Abolition of Slavery," by Bayard Tuckerman, with a preface, by John Jay, appears a letter dating 1852, written by Judge William Jay to his

William Jay

JAMES COOPER.
When a student at Yale.

grandson. This letter gives graphic glimpses of Yale College life during the student days there of its writer and James Cooper: " The resident graduates were denominated ' Sirs '; their place in Chapel was called ' the Sirs pew '; and when spoken of in college ' Sir ' was always placed before their names. At that time the freshmen occupied, in part, the place of sizers in the English universities, and they were required to run errands for the seniors. My room-mate was Sir Holly (Dr. Horace Holly). As a mere freshman, I looked up to my room-mate with great respect, and treated him accordingly. About half past five in winter, the bell summoned us from our beds, — I rose, generally, before six, — made the fire, and then went, pitcher in hand, often wading through snow, for water for Sir Holly and myself. Of the college bell," the letter continues: " at six it called us to prayers in the chapel. We next repaired to the recitation-rooms and recited, by candlelight, the lessons we had studied the preceding evening. At eight we had breakfast, — our meals were taken in a large hall with a kitchen opening into it. The students were arranged at tables according to their classes. All sat on wooden benches, not excepting the tutors; the latter had a table to themselves on an elevated platform whence they had a view of the whole company. But it was rather difficult for them to attend to their plates and to watch two hundred boys at the same time. Salt beef once a day, and dry cod were perhaps the most usual dishes. On Sunday mornings, during the winter, our breakfast-tables were graced with large tin milk-cans filled with stewed oysters; at the proper season we were occasionally treated with green peas. As you may suppose, a goodly number of waiters were needed in the hall. These were all students, and many of them among the best and most esteemed scholars. At nine the bell warned us to our rooms. At twelve it called us to a recitation or a lecture. After dinner we recommenced our studies for the third time, at four o'clock. During study hours the tutors would frequently go the rounds, looking into our rooms to see that we were not playing truant. Before supper, we all attended prayers in the chapel."

Although, from the necessity of his times, Chief-Justice John Jay was a slave owner, his son, William — refined, benevolent, pleasing in manner, but with a temper easily aroused by injustice — became an early, alert, and strong advocate of the anti-slavery cause. This eminent jurist who built his life upon the plan of his words, "Duties are ours and consequences are God's" (as did also Cooper), was graphically addressed and described by Cooper as "Thou most pugnacious man of peace."

Leaving Yale to the more studious, no doubt the young man enjoyed this brief period of home-life and the distinguished guests drawn by its hospitality to Otsego Hall. Yet even this could not for long hold him there. Perhaps he was influenced by what he heard from them of the great outside world, and he, too, wished to see what it was like. As a stepping-stone to a commission in the navy, Judge Cooper secured a berth for his son, who shipped as a sailor before-

OUTWARD BOUND.

the-mast in the *Stirling*, of Wiscasset, Maine, John Johnston master and part owner. In the care of a merchant, young Cooper went down to the docks to look about the ship and sign the articles, and the next day he returned in his sailor's garb. The *Stirling* was taken into the stream, and his new comrades, a mixture of nations, — four Americans, a Portuguese, a Spaniard, a Prussian, a Dane, an Englishman, a Scotch boy, and a Canadian, — tumbled aboard, not quite themselves; but by night they were in working trim. The young commander was described as "kind and considerate of all hands," and the ship as "carrying a motley crew." When "all hands" were called to get the *Stirling* under way, Cooper, with another boy, was sent aloft to loose the foretopsail. With eager will he tugged stoutly at "the robbins," when the second mate appeared just in time to prevent him from dropping his part of the sail into the top. The good-hearted mate had a kindly mind for the "new hand," and the men were too busy to notice small failures aloft. Young Cooper soon found an old salt who taught him to knot and splice with the best of them, and old Barnstable was repaid for these lessons by the merry times they had together when they got ashore. However, with her cargo of flour, the *Stirling* sailed from New York in the autumn of 1806 for the English market at Cowes, and therefore when Cooper should have been taking his class degree at Yale, he was outward bound on the sea's highway. Being to the manor born did not admit the sailor before-the-mast to the captain's cabin, but no doubt the long, rough voyage of forty stormy days did make of the young man a jolly tar. Through her usual veil of fog came Cooper's first view of Old England when threatened with Napoleon's invasion. Forty-odd sail of warships were sighted by the night-watch when the *Stirling* passed the straits of Dover at daybreak. They gave the young man an object-lesson that he never forgot, in the watchfulness and naval power of Great Britain. The *Stirling* had but dropped anchor in English waters when she was boarded by a British man-of-war's boat-crew, and one of her best hands was forced into the English navy service, and another sailor barely escaped, he having satisfactory papers. At London a third hand was lost, and Captain Johnston himself was seized by a press-gang.

Finally, in round-jacket and tarpaulin, the

future guest of Samuel Rogers and Holland
House, planted his feet on British soil. At
London he saw about everything a gay young
fellow of seventeen in sailor's gear could, of that
wonderful city, — or so thought Ned Myers, one
of his shipmates, who was with him most of the
time. Concerning these jaunts Myers says: " I
had one or two cruises of a Sunday in the tow
of Cooper, who soon became a branch pilot in
those waters about the parks and the West End,
the Monument, St. Paul's and the lions; Cooper
took a look at the arsenal, jewels, and armory
[Tower of London]. He had a rum time of
it in his sailor's rig; hoisted in a wonderful lot
of gibberish." And with his fine stories of each
day's sights in old London town, the young sailor
would make merry evenings for his forecastle

GIBRALTAR.

[45]

comrades, of whom it is recorded his strength could lay flat on their backs in two minutes.

In January the *Stirling* spread her sails for another stormy passage, — to the straits of Gibraltar. On running out, the ship was boarded by a gun-boat officer, who tried to press a Swede; whereupon, young Cooper thinking it an insult to our flag, began high words with the Englishman, but was soon silenced by Captain Johnston. The *Stirling* met with various stirring adventures, being chased by a Bay-of-Biscay pirate and rescued by the timely appearance of a British cruiser. It was thick westerly weather when they ran into the straits, and as the English fleet was off Cape Trafalgar, Captain Johnston realized the danger of being run down in the night, and came on deck during the middle watch for a sharp lookout on the forecastle. Night orders were given when came the warning, " Sail ho! " and through the mists and shadows was seen dimly a two-decker bearing directly down upon them. The Captain ordered the helm " hard up! " and called Cooper to " bring a light." With a leap he rushed to the cabin, seized the light, and in half a minute it was swinging from the mizzen rigging, his promptness saving the ship. So near were the two vessels that the deck officer's voice was distinctly heard calling his quarter-master to "port the helm." As the great mass swept by them she seemed about to crush their railing with the muzzle of her guns.

While the *Stirling* was lying off the old Moorish town of Almaria, Cooper and others were sent ashore in a jolly-boat to boil pitch. To return to the ship they put off in a heavy sea, knowing it would be difficult to work through the surf; but orders were orders, and delay would not help. So off they plunged, when suddenly a breaker " took the bow of the boat, and lifting her almost on end, turned her keel uppermost." All hands got safely ashore — how, none could tell. A second launching resulted as the first, but with a third they succeeded in forging their way out, and boarded the ship. Later they ran short of provisions. But the *Stirling's* return cargo was brought back safely to London, where the ship lay at anchor for two months or more, and then sailed in July for America. After a voyage of fifty-two days she dropped anchor at Philadelphia, September 18, 1807. So much for this good ship named for Stirling Castle of Bonnie Scotland.

Such were the lessons young Cooper learned in

this rough but manly school. A brother officer who knew him well said, " He was active, prompt, and efficient, a pleasant shipmate, always ready to do his duty, and rigorous too in exacting it of others." Of Cooper's " Naval History " was added, " It is the noblest tribute ever paid to a noble profession." Aboard the *Stirling* on these several cruises Cooper learned much that afterwards appeared in his sea tales. It was of this sea-service that he wrote, " I have been myself one of eleven hands, officers included, to navigate a ship of three hundred tons across the Atlantic Ocean; and, what is more, we often reefed topsails with the watch." Of the *Stirling* he wrote, " The ship was on a bow-line most of the time "; and he thought her " one of the wettest ships that ever floated when heading up against the sea." A lively account of this eleven months' service is found in Cooper's story of " Ned Myers." This life of his shipmate aboard the *Stirling* was written in 1843. The old salt was a battered hulk in the " Sailor's Snug Harbor " when Cooper was on the crest of the wave of his literary fame, and the old sailor, wondering if this Cooper could be the comrade of his youth in the *Stirling* days of yore, wrote, after

SAILOR'S SNUG HARBOR.

the twenty-five years of separation, to inquire.
The answer was, "I am your old shipmate,
Ned." Later, "Ned" was invited to visit the
Hall. Many remember the interesting two in
1843. "Hardly a day passed that they were
not seen, as the heavy Hall gates swung open
at eleven o'clock, coming out for a morning walk
or a sail on the lake; — Cooper's portly form,
and by his side a shriveled figure with halting
step, leaning heavily on a crooked stick which
served for a cane. They were as strong in contrast as it was possible for men to be." It was
during this visit that the old sailor spun his life-
yarn in his own way and Cooper wove it into
his book, "Ned Myers."

[49]

Perhaps the following interesting Cooperstown story of Cooper's youth is of the time of his return from his *Stirling* voyage. One day a merry group of young men proposed a foot-race, the course to be around the square — a distance of about one hundred yards. James Cooper was named as one of the runners, and his rival was soon chosen. According to custom, the village boys, girls, men, and women were spectators. Like a mettlesome steed in curb young Cooper looked at the wager, — a basket of fruit, — then at his race-mate, and accepted the challenge, but not on even terms. It was not enough for a sailor simply to outrun a landsman; he could do more. A little girl stood near, her bright face eager with watching

OTSEGO HALL GATES.

for the fray. Cooper turned quickly and caught her up in his arms, and with the pride and muscle of an athlete exclaimed, " I 'll carry her with me and beat you! " Away they flew, Cooper with his laughing burden upon his shoulders; one corner was turned, and the excited crowd saw with surprise James Cooper with his small rider keeping pace with the other flying youth. Another, and the other corners were soon passed; both sprang like race-horses near the end of the course, but Cooper, with his little black-eyed girl aloft and the perspiration pouring down his manly brow and cheeks, was the first to reach the mark, and amidst such cheers and hurrahs as only pioneers can freely give, and as freely enjoy. The fruit he had won, but soon it was shared by all around. That little girl, later the wife of Captain William Wilson, often told the story of her ride on pleasant James Cooper's shoulders.

While never a rhymester, Cooper, in his early manhood and at rare times after, did write occasional sentimental and comic verses that betokened both clever imagination and other merit. Into the *Otsego Herald* printing-office a poor epileptic ballad-singer came one day to ask help

from a group of gentlemen. A purse was made
up for him, but he, looking among them, said if
one of them would write for him " a few verses
— something new " — they would be worth more

BUFFALO BURNT.

than the silver given him. Young Cooper offered to try, and asked on what subject he should
write. " There's nothing sells like ballads," was
the reply. So the ballad was promised; and
some thirty or more pathetic verses were written at once, about the small frontier village re-
cently burnt by troops under Colonel Murray
during the close of the last war with England.
This ballad bore the high-sounding title of " Buffalo Burnt, or the Dreadful Conflagration." It
won such success among the farm-house gentry

that the singer returned for another ballad and obtained it. Some years later Mr. Cooper was invited to a tea-party in a near village, when a young lady, led to the piano for music, began to

THE *VESUVIUS.*

sing, much to the author's disturbing amazement, "Buffalo Burnt, or the Dreadful Conflagration."

So passed the pleasant vacation days of our young sailor, whose training before-the-mast enabled his father to obtain for him a midshipman's commission in the United States Navy, for which James Cooper reported for duty at New York City, January 12, 1808. At the age of nineteen he first served aboard the *Vesuvius.* Thence he was ordered to Oswego, New York, to build the brig *Oneida* for Lake Ontario service, and which the spring of 1809 saw launched.

While the war flurries which called for the building of the vessel were tethered, Cooper had learned his lesson in ship-building, ship-yard duties, and water-border life; and these served

ONTARIO FORESTS.

him more than thirty years later in his matchless Indian story, "The Pathfinder." Miss Susan Cooper has left some interesting pages of this period of her father's naval service; in part they read: "In 1808 several young officers under Lieutenant Woolsey were ordered to the shores of Lake Ontario for building a small vessel of war. Among them was Mr. Cooper, then a midshipman in the service. Their road lay for many a mile through the forest to the mouth of the Oswego River, — their destination, — where the *Oneida*, a brig mounting sixteen guns, was built and launched. They enjoyed the wild coloring of frontier life. They roamed the forests and explored the shores in leisure hours. Cruises among the Thousand Islands were fre-

THE THOUSAND ISLANDS.

quent; many were the fine fish caught and good chowders eaten. The picturesque beauties of the region, the countless islands, were greatly enjoyed and never forgotten by the young midshipman." The youthful officers were ordered to Buffalo, and stopping for the night at a rude frontier inn, it was Cooper's duty to inquire what they might have for supper. " Mine host shook his head ruefully; he could promise very little. ' Give us what you eat yourself; you must

[55]

have food of some kind,' said Cooper. Mine host looked melancholy; on his honor he assured the young officers he had absolutely nothing to set before them but game, steak, and brook-trout; and, maybe his wife could find cranberries for a tart! A month earlier they should have had a dish of fried pork fit for the President, with a

THE PORT OF BUFFALO.

pumpkin pie after it. 'Game's plenty, but nothin' else!' added the publican with a sigh. Mine host was pining for pork! On this expedition Mr. Cooper saw Niagara for the first time. He was struck with the grandeur of the cataract, but felt its sublime character far more deeply on a later visit — after his return from Europe."

When the *Oneida* was launched the gallant

young officers resolved to celebrate the event by giving a ball. " This was an enterprise of a desperate character; — building a brig hundreds

CAPTAIN M. T. WOOLSEY.

of miles from a ship-yard was a trifle to giving a ball in the wilderness. True, one fiddle and half a dozen officers were something; refreshments and a military ball-room might be hoped for; but where, pray, were the ladies to come from?" They would not think of dancing with each other, and ladies must be found. Vigorous efforts were made by sending boats in some directions and carts miles in others, to invite the ladies; and they accepted. As the hour drew near a very delicate point came up for decision — the honors due different fair claimants. After a council of war, Lieutenant Woolsey gave to his master-of-ceremonies these orders: " All ladies, sir, provided with shoes and stockings are to be led to the head of the Virginia reel; ladies with shoes, and without stockings, are considered in the second rank; ladies without shoes or stockings you will lead, gentlemen, to the foot of the country dance!" Such was a grand military ball in Oswego County in 1808–9.

About this time occurred an amusing incident of their raw young mess-servant, fresh from Ireland: " A table-cloth had taken fire and was in full blaze; Paddy was at the moment filling a teapot from an ample kettle in his hand. ' Pour the water on the table!' called out one of the officers. ' Sure, the wather is *hot*, your honor!' exclaimed Paddy, in great dismay, holding the kettle at a very safe distance from the blazing cloth, and his face such a picture of helpless despair as to make Mr. Cooper heartily laugh at every after-thought of it."

The passing of thirty or more years made of this light-hearted young midshipman a well-known writer, with the purpose that his next book should tell of this unforgettable region of the great lakes. He wished to bring into it the sailors and Indians as, by coming in close contact with them, " he knew their personalities and characteristics." Then, forest scenes without

"Natty Bumppo" could scarce come from his
pen after the drawings of old "Leatherstocking" of "The Pioneers," "Hawkeye" of "The
Mohicans," and the "aged trapper" of "The
Prairie." So it came about that "Natty, the
lover," stepped into these pages — Natty, "so
simple, so tender, so noble and true — what shall
be said of him? We must all needs love him; it
is not with words but with tears that we wring

THE PATHFINDER.

his hand and part from him on the lake shore"
as "The Pathfinder." Glowing and brave proved

A BUBBLE OF A BOAT.

his Mabel, as " the bubble of a boat floated on the
very crest of a foaming breaker," — yet not for
him. But the ripple of the lake's waves and rust-
ling of forest leaves are as unforgettable as the
low, sweet tones of " Dew-of-June." Of " The
Pathfinder " and Cooper Balzac wrote: " Its interest is tremendous. He surely owed us this
masterpiece after the last two or three raphso-
dies he has given us."

In the year 1809 Cooper was attached to a
gun-boat serving on Lake Champlain, and on
November 13 following, he was ordered to the
Wasp, under Capt. James Lawrence, of Bur-

The *Wasp*.

lington — a personal friend, and also the heroic commander of the *Chesapeake* in her action with the *Shannon*, in which his last words were, " Don't give up the ship! " It was aboard the *Wasp* that Cooper's lifelong friendship with Commodore Shubrick of South Carolina began, who, like himself, and a year younger, was a midshipman. To this friend the author dedicated " The Pilot," " Red Rover," and other stories.

Political feeling ran high in those early days of 1809, and prominent persons did not escape from their opponents with bitter feeling only. So it came about that in December of that year, Judge Cooper, on leaving a hot convention, met his death, — the result of a blow on the head, as he was coming down the steps of the State capitol at Albany, New York. No one of his day who was engaged in the work of large buying and selling of land made so deep an impression as did Judge Cooper on his times, and on his author son, whose land books disclose to posterity with historic exactness the hardships and values of the pioneers of our country.

After Judge Cooper's death Richard Fenimore, his eldest son, became the head of the family, and it was to him that James wrote from

I wrote you yesterday, a letter in a great hurry, as its contents are of some importance. I employ the leisure time offered today, to inform you more fully of my views.

When you were in the City, I hinted to you, my intention of resigning at the end of this session of Congress, should nothing be done for the Navy — my only reason at that time was the blasted prospects of the service. I accordingly wrote my resignation and as usual offer'd it to Capt. Lawrence, for his inspection — he very warmly recommended to me to give the service the trial of another year or two — at the same time offering to procure me a furlough which would leave me perfect master of my actions in the interval — I thought it wisest to accept this proposition — at the end of this year I have it in my power to resign, should the situation of the Country warrant it.

Like all the rest of the sons of Adam, I have bowed to the influence of the claims of a fair damsel of eighteen. I loved her like a man and told her of it like a sailor. The peculiarity of my situation occasion'd me to act with something like precipitancy. I am perfectly confident, however, I shall never have cause to repent of it — . As you are *cooly* to decide, I will as *cooly* give you the qualities of my mistress. Susan De Lancey is the daughter of a man of very respectable connections and a handsome fortune — amiable, sweet-tempered and happy in her disposition. — She has been educated in the country, occasionally trying the temperature of the City — to rub off the rust — but hold a moment, it is enough she pleases *me* in

[63]

the qualities of her *person* and *mind* — . Like a true
quixotic lover, I made proposals to her father — he has
answered them in the most gentlemanly manner — .
You have my consent to address my daughter if you
will gain the approbation of your mother — He also
informs me that his daughter has an estate in the
County of Westchester in reversion, secured to her by
a deed in trust to him — . I write all this for *you* —
you know *I* am indifferent to anything of this nature.
Now I have to request — you will take your hat and
go to mother, the boys, girls, and say to them have you
any objection that James Cooper shall marry at a
future day, Susan De Lancey. If any of them forbid
the bans may the Lord have forgiven them — for I
never will — . Then take your pen and write to Mr.
De Lancey stating the *happiness* and *pleasure* it will
give all the family to have this connection completed
— all this I wish you to do immediately, as I am de-
prived of the pleasure of visiting my flame until this
is done, by that confounded *bore*, delicacy — be so
good as to inclose the letter in one to me, at the same
time don't forget to inclose a handsome sum to square
the yards here and bring me to Cooperstown.

I wish not to interrupt you in your attempt to clear
the estate — my expenditure shall be as small as
possible.   *Your brother,*   JAMES COOPER.

The de Lanceys were Huguenots and their
loyalty to England during the Revolution
made several of them British officers. Although Cooper was ever a staunch American,

this incident, with several others in his later life, seemed unfavorable to some few who were only too willing to question his loyalty.

Miss de Lancey's great grandfather, Stephen,

FRAUNCES TAVERN.

JAMES DE LANCEY'S SEAL.

THE HEATHCOTE ARMS.

was the first of this aristocratic Westchester-County family on American soil. He fled from Normandy on the revocation of the edict of Nantes, and in 1686 came to New York. Here his son James became chief-justice and lieuten-

[65]

Caleb Heathcote,

ant-governor, and married Ann, eldest daughter of the Hon. Caleb Heathcote, lord of the manor of Scarsdale, Westchester, and whose manor house was Heathcote Hill, which their fourth son, John Peter de Lancey, Cooper's father-in-law, inherited from his mother. One of a number of services the old-world Derbyshire Heathcote-Hill family rendered to its country was giving to the Bank of England its first president. The de Lancey name still clings to

FRAUNCES TAVERN LONG ROOM.

the new-world history in Fraunces Tavern, built
by Stephen de Lancey in 1700, for his home.
Sixty-two years later it became the tavern of
Samuel Fraunces. In 1776 and 1783 it was the
headquarters of General Washington, and in its
famous *Long Room* " The Father of his Country " made his farewell address, and bid adieu
to his generals. Number 130 Broadway was the
de Lancey home of 1730, and here was given the
first inauguration ball of our nation. On this
site was built " Burn's Coffee House," which
teemed with interesting events. The City Hotel
took its place in 1806. John Peter de Lancey
married Elizabeth, daughter of Col. Richard
Floyd, and in 1789 came to Heathcote Hill,
Westchester County, which he rebuilt on the

site of the old manor house, burned down. In
this home he lived out his days. Here his son,
William Heathcote, Bishop of Western New

BURN'S COFFEE HOUSE.

York, was born; and also his lovely daughter,
Susan Augusta; here she was wooed and won
by the handsome young naval officer, and on New
Year's day, 1811, became Mrs. James Cooper.
In 1899 Dr. Theodore F. Wolfe writes of Cooper
and Heathcote Hill — that some of the great
trees which waved their green leafage above him
lingering here with sweetheart or bride yet shade
the grounds, but the household that welcomed
him and gave him a beloved daughter lie in a
little grass-grown cemetery near to this old home.
Mrs. Cooper had a sweet, gracious way of guid-

ing by affection her husband, and he gave her
his heart's devotion through the forty years of

HEATHCOTE HILL.

their happily mated life. Cooper and his young
bride began life by playing a game of chess between the ceremony and supper. Then, he driv-

ing two horses tandem, they made their wedding
journey to Cooperstown in a gig. His furlough
ended a few months later, and to please his

COOPER'S FENIMORE FARM HOUSE.

wife, he resigned in May from the navy. Long
afterwards he wrote, " She confesses she would
never have done for Lady Collingwood." For
a year or more Cooper and his wife lived with
her father at Heathcote Hill, Mamaroneck, New
York, and afterwards in a near-by cottage on
the " Neck," which Cooper named " Closet Hall "
because it was so small, and he described it as
the home of the Littlepage family in " Satanstoe."
Only two old willows remain of the group that
almost concealed Cooper's wee house, now entirely rebuilt, and they named the place as the
home of Alice B. Havens, who wrote here some
of her poems and stories — so Dr. Wolfe writes
of Closet Hall. After some brief housekeeping

in this "wee home," the young people again made a part of the family at Heathcote Hill, where they lived until 1814. Then, with the two little girls born to them, they went for a short time to Cooperstown, and thence to their Fenimore farm of some one hundred and fifty acres along Otsego's southwestern shores. "On a rising knoll overlooking lake and village a handsome stone house was begun for their life home." The near-by hill, called Mount Ovis, pastured the Merino sheep which he brought into the country. He loved his gardening, and was active for the public good, serving as secretary of the county Agricultural Society, and also of the Otsego County Bible Society. In the full flush of youth and its pleasures there were the pleasant diversions of driving, riding, and rowing. So lived flute-playing Cooper, brave and handsome, at twenty-five.

Cooper's mother was then living with her older sons at Otsego Hall, and it is recorded that " she took great delight in flowers, and the end of the long hall was like a green-house, in her time "; that " she was a great reader of romances; a marvelous housekeeper, and beautifully nice and neat in her arrangements: her flower-garden at the south of the house was considered something wonderful in variety of flowers." Between her Old-Hall home and the families of her children, — Richard's on " Apple Hill," Isaac's at " Edgewater," Nancy's at the " Old Stone House," and James's at " Fenimore," — these years were full of charm and interest for them all, which later became sweet and enduring memories. Sadness crept in, through the loss of James's daughter Elizabeth; but two more came to lift this shadow in the Fenimore home.

In 1817 Cooper and his young family started for a few month's visit to Heathcote Hill, and later in this year he lost his mother. As the stone house, then building at Fenimore, burned down in 1823, the land was sold later, and the few months' expected absence grew into seventeen years. Perhaps it was this thread of loss added to his wife's wishes that led Cooper to build a country home on the Scarsdale farm, — a portion of the de Lancey estate, which came to Mrs. Cooper after her marriage. Here he built the picturesque home in which his literary career began. " Nothing that Cooper knew remains excepting the superb land and water view," which drew him to place this home of his

Elizabeth Fenimore Cooper in the Old Hall Home.

COOPER'S ANGEVINE FARM HOME.

there, and he has pictured mile upon mile of the
shimmering, sail-dotted Sound in scenes of his
"Water Witch." It is of record that the windows of the room in which he wrote "Precaution," "The Spy," and "The Pioneers" overlooked this enchanting vista which then and later
claimed place in his books. It was four miles
from Mamaroneck and some twenty-five from
New York City. The height on which the new
house stood was called Angevine, from a former
Huguenot tenant. It gave a glorious view over

miles of fine wooded country, with a broad reach of Long Island Sound beyond, over which were moving white, glittering sails "a sailor's eye loves to follow." Of active habits and vigorous health, Cooper threw himself with almost boyish eagerness into the improvement and beautifying of this homestead, — planning the barn, building the then new zigzag, ha-ha fence, watching the growth of shrubs and trees that he had transplanted, and with cheering talk lightening the labors of his workmen.

"In 1818 Cooper was made paymaster, and in the next year quartermaster in the Fourth Division of Infantry, New York State Militia. As Governor Clinton's aid, in blue and buff uni-

MAMARONECK CREEK SLOOPS.

form, cocked hat, and sword, and title of colonel, he would go to reviews on his favorite horse, ' Bull-head.' "

At that time each village on the Sound had its sloop which carried the farmer's produce thrice a week through the perils of Hell Gate to Fulton market, and brought back tea, sugar, cloth, calicoes, and silks, and, perchance, some volume fresh from the London press, — a bit of Byron's brilliance, a romance from the unknown author of " Waverley," one of Miss Edgeworth's charming tales, or the more serious religious work of Wilberforce — which had " arrived by packet-ship from England " — the next day's papers would announce. Lucky was thought the household that could first cut the pages of the new print.

Reading, which always enters so naturally into country life, made pleasant their even-ing hours and rainy days at Angevine. Mr. Cooper was a fine reader. His voice was deep, clear, and expressive, and during those quiet country evenings he often read aloud to one " who listened with affectionate interest through a long life," and he read to her with special pleasure. For Shakespeare he was always ready. Pope,

Thompson, and Gray were also in favor, but not more than a page or two at a time of Milton. He thought that Shakespeare should have written " Paradise Lost." " He took the greatest delight in the ' Waverley ' novels, and never doubted they were written by Walter Scott, the poet. On one occasion a new novel chanced to lie on the table and he was asked to read it. The title and look of the book were not to his taste; he opened it, however, and began. Suddenly, after reading through a few pages, it was thrown aside in disgust: ' I can write a better book than that myself! ' was his exclamation." Mrs. Cooper laughed at the absurd idea that he, who disliked writing even a letter, should write a book, and playfully challenged him to make good his word; and when urged to begin, he at once outlined a tale of English high-life. As the story grew, the writer became interested, and before long the first pages of Cooper's first book, " Precaution, or Prevention is Better than Cure," were written. When finished, much to his amazement, Mrs. Cooper further urged him to publish it; so, with the manuscript, they set out in their gig to seek counsel of the Jays at Bedford, and other friends, who approved. " One lady, not

John Jay

in the secret, felt sure she had read it before."
It was published, without the author's name,
August 25, 1820, and was credited to an English woman. A. T. Goodrich, the publisher, surprised the public by declaring it the work of an
American gentleman of New York. It was soon
republished in England, and claimed the attention usually accorded that style of book in its
day. Whatever of its worth, the work had
awakened Cooper's powers; and its modest success in a field new to him led his friends to urge
him to write on subjects that were in near touch
with his daily life. None knew better than he
the frontier and sea-faring life of his own and

earlier times. So, then, for home-country subjects, and thinking it would be his last attempt, he exclaimed, " I will write another book!" and soon decided on patriotism as its *motif*. At this period many were the visits to Judge Jay's Westchester home at Bedford. The house, part of wood and part of stone, had a spacious, comfortable piazza along its front. The interior had more of cheerfulness than of elegance, but a great air of abundance, and was a peaceful shelter for the waning days of that eminent statesman and patriot. Of this household Cooper wrote later: " I scarcely remember to have mingled with any family where there was a more happy union of quiet decorum and high courtesy

BEDFORD HOUSE.

than I met with beneath the roof of Mr. Jay."
To no place more fitting than his wistaria-cov-
ered library could Cooper have gone for patriotic
inspiration. The venerable Judge, as he smoked

THE LIBRARY AT BEDFORD HOUSE.

his long clay pipe, used to delight in telling anecdotes of the Revolution, " the truth of which,"
he said, " never had been and never would be
written."

One summer afternoon, while sitting on his
broad piazza under the lindens, Cooper, with
others, listened to the Judge's recital of the story
of a spy's great struggles and unselfish loyalty
while serving his country in the American Revolution, and the story gave Cooper an idea for
his " Harvey Birch." The fact that strolling

peddlers, staff in hand and pack on back, were common visitors then at country houses, became another aid. "It was after such a visit of a Yankee peddler of the old sort, to the cottage at Angevine, that Harvey's lot in life was decided — he was to be a spy and a peddler." It was something to the author's after regret that he drew the dignity of George Washington into the "Harper" of this story.

"The entire country between the Americans on the skirts of the Highlands and the British on Manhattan — or 'the Neutral Ground' — suffered more in harried skirmishes, pillage, violence, fire, and the taking of life itself, than any of its extent during this strife." Scarsdale and Mamaroneck were in this region, with White

HARVEY BIRCH'S CAVE.

[81]

Plains close by. Fort Washington was on a near height, and Dobb's Ferry a few miles off. " The Coopers' daily drive from Angevine discovered a pretty thicket, some swampy land, and a cave in which to hide the loyal, to be fed by friendly hands at night until escape was possible. There were also at hand the gloomy horrors of a haunted wood where gliding ghosts fought midnight battles " — all of this the farmers *knew* and could tell of, too. One of them, " Uncle John," lived just below the home hill in a wee cot of four walls, each of a different color — red, yellow, brown, and white. He frequently came up the Angevine-home hill to tell, between his apples, nuts, and glasses of cider, tales of what he, too, *knew*, to a good listener, — the master of the house. Then there was " Major Brom B., a hero of the great war, with his twenty-seven martial spirits, all uniformed in silver gray, his negro Bonny and his gun, ' the Bucanneer,' had not its fellow on the continent." These were all aids, and sources of unfailing interest about the many Westchester chimney firesides of that day. In his " Literary Haunts and Homes," Dr. Theodore F. Wolfe tells of a fine, old-time home, beyond the valley below Cooper's Angevine farm, where he placed many an exciting scene of this coming tale. In 1899 Dr. Wolfe notes the house as changed, only by a piazza across its front,

THE LOCUSTS OF COOPER'S TIME AND OF TO-DAY.

from the days when Cooper knew it well, and that it was pleasantly shaded by many of the fine, tall trees that gave it the name of " The Locusts," which it kept in his story as the home of the Whartons. The descendants of the family he used to visit still live there, and one of them showed Dr. Wolfe all that was left of " The Four Corners," Betty Flanigan's hotel, whence Harvey Birch, Cooper's hero, escaped in Betty's petticoats. Cooper made these familiar scenes of southern New York the background of his second book, " The Spy, a Tale of the Neutral Ground," which also was published, without the

[83]

author's name, December 22, 1821. Its success called for a new edition the following March, and its translation into many foreign tongues. Of Cooper's " Betty Flanigan " Miss Edgeworth declared, " An Irish pen could not have drawn her better." Except Irving's " Sketch Book," his " Knickerbocker's History of New York," and Bryant's thin volume of eight poems, there were few books by native writers when " The Spy " appeared; and " then it was that the new world awakened to the surprising discovery of her first *American* novelist. The glory that Cooper justly won was reflected on his country, of whose literary independence he was the pioneer. ' The Spy ' had the charm of reality; it tasted of the soil." While the American press was slow to admit the merit of " The Spy," a cordial welcome was given the book in " The Port Folio." It was written by Mrs. Sarah Hall, mother of the editor, and author of " Conversations on the Bible." This act of timely kindness Cooper never forgot. June 30, 1822, Washington Irving, from London, wrote Mr. John E. Hall, the editor: " ' The Spy ' is extremely well spoken of by the best circles, — not a bit better than it deserves, for it does the author great credit."

THE SPY

A TALE OF THE NEUTRAL GROUND

"Stand or Die."

PHILADELPHIA

Published by Harrison Hall.

1822.

TITLE-PAGE OF THE FIRST EDITION OF "THE SPY."

In 1826, when " The Spy " was before the foot-
lights in Lafayette Theatre, on Broadway, near
Canal Street, Enoch Crosby, the supposed origi-

Enoch Crosby

nal spy, appeared in a box with friends, and
" was given thunders of applause." From " Portraits of Cooper's Heroines," by the Rev. Ralph
Birdsall of Cooperstown, is gleaned: On the
walls of the Newport home of the Rev. John
Cornell hang two old portraits that have close
connection with the inner history of " The Spy."
To their present owner they came from the New
York home of his mother, the late Mrs. Isaac

LAFAYETTE THEATRE.

Cornell, and to her they came from the Somerville, New Jersey, home of her father, Mr. Richard Bancker Duyckinck, who in his turn received them from his aunt, Mrs. Peter Jay, — the subject of one of these portraits and at one time mistress of the Jay mansion at Rye. Over one hundred years ago it was that, from the walls of this rare old home at Rye, Westchester County, the grace of these ladies on canvas caught James Cooper's thought to use them, by description, in his coming book, "The Spy." Chapter XIII describes closely the personal ap-

[87]

pearance and style of dress of these portraits.
"Jeanette Peyton," the maiden aunt of Cooper's
story, owes her mature charm to the portrait of
Mary Duyckinck, wife of Peter Jay. From the
"cap of exquisite lawn and lace," her gown of
rich silk, short sleeves and "large ruffles" of
lace which with "the experience of forty years,"
also veiled her shoulders, to the triple row of
large pearls about her throat, — all these details
are found in Cooper's text-picture of Jeanette
Peyton. His "Sarah Wharton" no less closely
follows the portrait of Mrs. Jay's older sister,
Sarah Duyckinck, who became Mrs. Richard
Bancker. Her name Sarah may have been given
purposely to Sarah Wharton of Cooper's story.
Cooper was thirty-two when it was written, and
it is not unlikely that Mrs. Jay, then eighty-five
years of age, was pleased with this delicate tribute the young novelist paid to the beauty of her
own and her sister's youth.

Four daughters and a son now shared the
author's home life, and in order to place his
little girls in a school and be near his publishers,
Cooper rented a modest brick house on Broadway, across the street from Niblo's Garden, near
No. 585, Astor's home, which was a grand resort

MARY DUYCKINCK, MRS. PETER JAY.   SARAH DUYCKINCK, MRS. RICHARD BANCKER.

of Halleck and Irving, who wrote there a part of his "Life of Washington." Cooper's house

WINDHURST'S NOOK, UNDER THE PARK THEATRE.

was just above Prince Street — then almost out of town.

The modern club being then unknown, the brilliant men of the day met in taverns, and there talked of "everything under the starry scope of heaven." In the 1820's there was Edward Windhurst's famous nook under the sidewalk below Park Theatre, where Edmund Kean, Junius Brutus Booth, Cooper, Morris, Willis, and Halleck made gay and brilliant talk.

In the "Life and Letters of Fitz-greene Halleck," by General James Grant Wilson, it appears that Cooper was warmly attached to Halleck

JAMES FENIMORE COOPER, 1822. From a photograph of the J. W. Jarvis portrait.

since 1815, when they first met. Fitz-greene Halleck is credited with taking Cooper's earliest books to Europe in 1822 and finding a London publisher for them. The novelist called his friend

FITZ-GREENE HALLECK. JOSEPH RODMAN DRAKE.

" The Admirable Croaker," on account of a series of amusing and satirical verses written by Halleck and Drake and published over the signature of " Croaker and Co.," in the public press of that day. Into this atmosphere of charm came delightful and delighting Joseph Rodman Drake, with his " six feet two " of splendid youth; he was thought by some " the handsomest man in New York." From out this brilliant group comes the record that " ' Culprit Fay,' written in

CRO' NEST.

August, 1816," says Halleck, "came from Cooper, Drake, DeKay, and Halleck, speaking of Scottish streams and their inspiration for poetry. Cooper and Halleck thought our American rivers could claim no such tribute of expression. Drake differed from his friends and made good his stand by producing in three days 'The Culprit Fay' from the Highlands of the Hudson; but," is added, "the Sound from Hunt's Point, his familiar haunt of *salt* water, made his inspiration."

To the City Hotel came Morris again with Dana, Cooper, and his friend, Samuel Woodworth, author of "The Old Oaken Bucket" —

SAMUEL WOODWORTH.   THE OLD OAKEN BUCKET.

to plan "The Mirror," in 1823. The story of the old song's writing is: At noon on a summer's day in 1817 Woodworth, whose pen-name was "Selim," walked home to dinner from his office at the foot of Wall Street. Being very warm, he drank a glass of water from his pump, and after drinking it said, "How much more refreshing would be a draught from the old bucket that hung in my father's well!" Then his wife — whom the poet called his inspiration — exclaimed, "Why, Selim, would n't that be a pretty subject for a poem?" Thus urged, he began writing at once, and in an hour's time finished the heart-stirring song so well known as

" The Old Oaken Bucket." At this City Hotel
Cooper himself in 1824 founded " The Bread
and Cheese Club " — so named because member-
ship was voted *for* with bits of bread, and *against*
with bits of cheese. He called it the " Lunch."
Later on, the " Lunch, or Cooper's Club," met
in Washington Hall, corner of Broadway and
Chambers Street. Among its distinguished mem-
bers were Chancellor Kent, DeKay, naturalist,
King, later president of Columbia College, the
authors Verplanck, Bryant, and Halleck, Morse
the inventor, the artists Durand and Jarvis, and
Wiley the publisher. They met Thursday evenings, each member in turn caring for the supper,
always cooked to perfection by Abigail Jones —
an artist of color, in that line. It was at one
of these repasts that Bryant " was struck with
Cooper's rapid, lively talk, keen observation,
knowledge, and accurate memory of details."
Said he: " I remember, too, being somewhat
startled, coming as I did from the seclusion of
a country life, with a certain emphatic frankness of manner, which, however, I came at last
to like and admire." Many an attractive page
might be written of these talks with Mathews,
rambles with DeKay, and daily chats with his

old messmates of the sea, and this " Bread and Cheese Club." Cooper was scarcely in France before he sent frequent missives to his friends at the club to be read at their weekly meetings; but it " missed its founder, went into a decline, and not long afterward quietly expired." General Wilson says that it was at Wiley's, corner of Wall and New Streets, in a small back room christened by Cooper " The Den " — which appeared over the door — that he first met " The Idle Man," R. H. Dana. Here Cooper was in the habit of holding forth to an admiring audience, much as did Christopher North about the same time in " Blackwood's " back parlor in George Street, Edinburgh.

John Bartlett's Bookshop, too, — " a veritable treasury of literary secrets," — in the new Astor House, became a haunt for the bookmen of its times. Cooper was fond of the society of literary men when he could meet them as *men*, and not as lions. He once said: " You learn nothing about a man when you meet him at a show dinner and he sits up to talk *for* you instead of talking *with* you. When I was in London Wordsworth came to town, and I was asked to meet him at one of those displays; but I would not

Trinity Church. City Hotel.

Washington Hall. Broadway & Reade St.

BLOCK ON WEST SIDE OF BROADWAY, BETWEEN PRINCE AND HOUSTON STREETS, 1823.

WEST SIDE OF BROADWAY, CORNER OF SPRING STREET, 1820.

BROADWAY IN COOPER'S TIME.

go." Then Mrs. Cooper said: "But you met him afterwards, my dear, and was very much pleased with him." To this Cooper replied: "Yes, at Rogers', and *was* very much pleased with him; but it was because I met him in a place where he felt at home, and he let himself out freely."

After some stay on Broadway, Cooper moved his family to their Beach Street abode. Some twenty paces from Hudson it stood, — a brick house of many attractions in the wrought iron railings, marble steps, arched doorway, high ceilings, with heavy, ornate mouldings, massive oaken doors, and Venetian blinds of the deep windows. Spacious and inviting was this city

home during the 1820's, in the fashionable district of St. John's. In April, 1823, while living here, Cooper was made a member of the Philadelphia Philosophical Society. August of this year he lost his first son, — the youngest child, — Fenimore; and he himself went through a serious illness, brought on by an accident: " On re-

No. 3 BEACH STREET, NEW YORK. ST. JOHN'S CHAPEL.

[99]

turning from a New Bedford visit his carriage broke down, and always glad to be afloat, he took passage in a sloop for New York. Being anxious to reach home, when the wind began to fail, and to make the most of the tide, he took the helm and steered the little craft himself through Hell Gate. The day was very stormy, and the trying heat brought on a sudden sun-stroke-like fever." February 3, 1824, his second son, Paul, was born.

"The Spy" finished and the glow of success upon its author, he again resolved "to try one more book." For this work his thoughts turned in love to the home of his childhood, so closely associated with the little "Lake of the Fields." "Green-belted with great forest trees was this 'smile of God' — from Mount Vision dreaming at its feet, to the densely wooded 'sleeping lion' guarding its head, nine miles to the north." Of the new book Cooper frankly said: "'The Pioneers' is written exclusively to please myself." Herein Leatherstocking makes his first appearance, and for all time, as Natty Bumppo, "with his silent footfall stepped from beneath the shadows of the old pines into the winter sunlight."

An old hunter — Shipman by name — often came with his rifle and dogs during the early years of the new colony, to offer his game at

OLD LEATHERSTOCKING.

William Cooper's door, and was a great attraction for the lads of Otsego Hall. A dim memory of Shipman served as an outline only for Cooper's creation, " Natty," as in strength and beauty of character he came from the writer's pen, to live through the five " Leather-stocking Tales," as " the ever familiar friend of boys." While Cooper placed no real character from life in this book, Judge Temple is accepted as a sketch of his father. The aim was to create a character from the class to which each belonged. Thus served brave old Indian John as " Chingachgook "; Mr. Grant, the missionary; and " Monsieur Le Quoi," the Frenchman. In " Chronicles of Cooperstown " it appears that a real " Mr. Le Quoy excited much interest in the place, in being superior to his occupation as a country grocer." One day a Mr. Renouard, a seaman, entered his shop for some tobacco, and returned in a few minutes agitated and pale, excitedly asking, " Who is the man that sold me this tobacco? " At the answer, " Mr. Le Quoy," he replied, " Yes, Mr. Le Quoy de Mesereau. When I went to Martinique to be port-captain of St. Pierre, this man was civil governor of the island, and refused to confirm my appointment." It was learned later that the French Revolution drove Mr. Le Quoy with little money to a New York friend, — a Mr. Murray, — who also knew well Judge Cooper, and they both advised this country store until peaceful France

could and did invite its owner to return to his
island home.

An Indian alarm of the early-village period
of 1794 formed the opening chapter of the new
book, but the incidents were mainly creations
of Cooper's fancy. Yet the pigeon-flights,
Natty's cave, which sheltered Elizabeth Temple
from the forest fire, and each charming picture of the Glimmerglass country, are true to
life. The academy, court-house, jail, inn; the
"'Cricket'—that famous old cannon which
sent its thunders thousands of times over the
Otsego hills on days of rejoicing—are fairly
given." The old gun was found when digging
the cellar of Judge Cooper's first house, and

NATTY'S CAVE.

[103]

James Clinton

was said to have been buried by troops under
Gen. James Clinton, who marched from Albany
against the Indians in 1779. They cut their
way through forests, brought their boats to
Lake Otsego, and their headquarters were in
a log house built on the future site of the first
Hall. The place where was the old Clinton Dam
is now marked by the Daughters of the American Revolution as the *one* Cooperstown, connecting link with the War of Independence.

CLINTON DAM.

The outward appearance of the old Hall is fairly given by Cooper's pen, but once within, all is a faithful record, "even to the severed nose of Wolfe, and the urn that held the ashes of Queen Dido." The tale was of a great landlord living among his settlers on property bearing his name. The book was "The Pioneers, or, Sources of the Susquehanna," and "thirty-five hundred copies sold before noon of the day it was published."

It was of "The Pioneers" that Bryant wrote: "It dazzled the world by the splendor of its novelty."

An interesting incident of Cooper's kindness of heart is of this date and some ten years later came to light as follows: After his return from Europe

[105]

in 1833 he one day gave to his eldest daughter " a small book bound in boards." It was entitled " Tales for Fifteen, or, Imagination and Heart " by Jane Morgan. He said to her: " Dearie, here is a little book that I wrote for Wiley," adding that he had bought it at a news stand on his way home. It appears " when Wiley failed a number of his patrons wrote stories and gave them to him." These two — one called " Heart " and the other " Imagination " were written by Cooper, but " curiously enough," — were published under the pen-name of " Jane Morgan." The book is very rare; only two copies are known to be in existence.

The thought of writing a romance of the sea first came to Mr. Cooper while dining at Mr. Charles Wilkes', where the table-talk turned on " The Pirate," just issued by the author of " Waverley." When his marine touches were highly praised for their accuracy, Cooper held they were not satisfactory to the nautical reader. His friends thought more accuracy might better please seamen but would prove dull reading for the general public. With his usual spirit, Cooper refused to be convinced, and on his way home that evening " the outlines of a nautical romance

were vaguely sketched in his mind "; but he
never dreamed it would become one of a series
of sea-stories. "I must write one more book

" TALES FOR FIFTEEN, OR IMAGINATION AND HEART."

— a sea tale — " he said, " to show what can
be done in this way by a sailor!" The stirring struggles of the American Revolution again
enlisted the author's loyal pen-service in the

character of that bold adventurer, John Paul Jones, and his cruise in *The Ranger*, when he made his daring descent upon Whitehaven and

St. Mary's Isle, which suggested to Cooper his plot for " The Pilot." Two ships, a frigate and the schooner *Ariel*, were drawn for the tale. During its writing the author had many doubts of its success. Friends thought the sea tame when calm, and unpleasant in storms; and as to ladies — the reading of storms would surely make them seasick. His first encouragement came from an Englishman of taste, though a doubter of American talent. To Cooper's surprise, this authority pronounced his sea tale good. Then came the favorable opinion of Commodore Shubrick, of which the author wrote: "Anxious to know what the effect would be on the public, I read a chapter to S——, now captain, which contained an account of a ship working off-shore in a gale. My listener betrayed interest as we proceeded, until he could no longer keep his seat. He paced the room furiously until I got through, and just as I laid down the paper he exclaimed: 'It is all very well, but you have let your jib stand too long, my fine fellow!' I blew it out of the bolt-rope in pure spite!" And thus it was that when the author "came beating out of the 'Devil's Grip,'" this old messmate jumped from his seat and paced the floor with strides, not letting a detail escape him. Cooper was fully satisfied and accepted the criticism, and the tale, alive with spirited description of sea-action, won the day. It was written with all the author's power and accuracy of detail. In "Mr. Gray" appeared John Paul Jones, while "Long Tom Coffin" was said to be Mr. Irish, the mate of the *Stirling*, in which the lad "Cooper made his voyage before-the-mast." Of this mate and the

Yankees the author wrote: "He too was from Nantucket, and was a prime fellow, and fit to command a ship." Prof. Brander Matthews calls this simple-hearted cockswain and Natty Bumppo "co-heirs of time." The famous fifth chapter of "The Pilot" was the first fiction to show that "a master of the sea tale had come into the world, and it has never been surpassed in literature of the sea." This, the third of Cooper's novels, won for him his greatest popularity. It was dedicated to William Branford Shubrick, United States Navy — the author's loyal friend since their days together on the *Wasp,* in 1809. Its inscription reads in part: "My Dear Shubrick — by your old Messmate, the Author." A few days after "The Pilot" was issued, January, 1824, Cooper wrote this friend: "I found Wiley had the book in the hands of his five printers — on my return — for reprint. So much for our joint efforts." Concerning "The Pilot" and its author, this appeared in the *Edinburgh Review:* "The empire of the sea is conceded to him by acclamation."

Meeting Cooper at dinner three months later, Bryant wrote his wife that "he seemed a little giddy with the great success his works have met." Another said: "What wonder that the hearty, breezy author of ' The Spy,' ' The Pioneers,' and ' The Pilot,' should, by a certain ' emphatic frankness of manner,' have somewhat startled the shy, retiring, country poet who had not yet found his place on *The Evening Post!*" Later, in 1824, to Richard Henry Dana's newsy letter about Cooper's foreign standing, Bryant replies: "What you tell me of the success of our countryman, Cooper, in England, is an omen of good things. I hope it is the breaking of a bright day for American literature." Bryant's memorial address after Cooper's death remains

LONG TOM COFFIN.

a splendid record of their unclouded friendship, based on mutual respect. It was delivered at Metropolitan Hall, in New York City, February 25, 1852. The occasion was honored by the presence of the most brilliant men of the time. Daniel Webster presided, assisted by William Cullen Bryant, and Washington Irving. At that time these three men were made the subjects of a pencil sketch by Daniel Huntington.

Mr. George Palmer Putnam thus describes a meeting between Irving and Cooper, after the latter's return from Europe: "One day Mr. Irving was sitting at my desk, with his back to the door, when Mr. Cooper came in (a little bustling as usual) and stood at the office entrance, talking. Mr. Irving did not turn (for obvious reasons), and Cooper did not see him. I had acquired caution as to introductions without mutual consent, but with brief thought — a sort of instinct — I stoutly obeyed the impulse of the moment, and simply said, 'Mr. Cooper, here is Mr. Irving.' The latter turned, Cooper held out his hand cordially, dashed at once into an animated conversation, took a chair, and, to my surprise and delight, the two authors sat for an hour, chatting in their best manner about

almost every topic of the day and former days;
and Mr. Irving afterwards frequently alluded

Bryant, Webster and Irving.

to the incident as being a very great gratifica-
tion to him. Not many months afterwards, he
sat on the platform and joined in Bryant's tribute to the genius of the departed novelist.

September 18, 1851, Irving wrote: "The
death of Fenimore Cooper is an event of deep
and public concern. To me it comes with a
shock; for it seems but the other day that I
saw him at Putnam's, in the full vigor of mind
and body, 'a very castle of a man.' He left
a space in our literature which will not be easily

[113]

supplied. I shall not fail to attend the proposed meeting."

It is recorded that " Yale never, in later years, saw fit to honor herself by giving Cooper his degree, but Columbia, in this instance more intelligent than either Harvard or Yale, in 1824, conferred on the author the honorary degree of A.M."

When, in 1824, General Lafayette, as the Nation's guest, landed from the *Cadmus* at Castle Garden, Mr. Cooper made one of the active committee of welcome and entertainment. Of his part in the Castle-Garden ball, and his enthusiasm, a friend wrote: " After working hard all day in preparations and all night in carrying them out, towards dawn he went to the office of his friend Charles King and wrote out a full and accurate report, which appeared in Mr. King's paper the next day." Concerning this famous Castle-Garden ball, Cooper himself wrote: " A tall spar was raised in the center, a vast awning of sail-cloth covered the whole, which was concealed by flags that gave a soft, airy finish — all flooded by lights. Music of the national air hailed Lafayette's arrival. The brilliant throngs and gay dancers over the floor

fell into line like a charm, forming a lane,
through which the old man passed, giving and
receiving warm and affectionate salutations at
every step to the small marquee in the midst,

THE LANDING OF LAFAYETTE, 1824.

prepared for the 'Guest of the Nation.' He
was like a father among his children." In
various other ways Cooper paid tributes of
courtesy to General Lafayette during this visit
to America.

As the three successful books which the author
had now written dealt with the strength and
struggles of liberty-loving Americans for their
new country, his wide sense of justice suggested
writing on loyalty from the other point of view
— the Mother Country's — as held by men of

birth and honor. This loyalty to England
Cooper made the subject of his next book. It
was a dangerous venture, and a time too near

LAFAYETTE AND THE BRANDYWINE VASE.

the dearly-bought laurels of our young republic
in its separation from England. But the author
made every effort for accuracy on all points;
he was tireless in his study of history, state
papers, official reports, almanacs, and weather-
records. A journey "to Yankee Land" familiar-

ized him with every locality he so faithfully
described in the pages of " Lionel Lincoln."
" A Legend of the Thirteen Republics " was an
added title to the first edition only (1825) of
" Lionel Lincoln," for Cooper's intention to

JOB PRAY.

write a story of each of the thirteen states was
given up later, and the title " A Narrative of
1775 " took its place. The author himself was
not satisfied with this work, nor with the character
of " Lionel Lincoln," whose lack of commanding interest makes " Job," his poor half-witted
brother and son of " Abigail," — a tenant of
the old warehouse, — the *real* hero of the book.
Of its author, Bancroft the historian wrote:
" He has described the battle of Bunker's Hill
better than it has ever been described in any
other work." Another high authority says:

[117]

The ATTACK on BUNKER's HILL, Burning of CHARLES TOWN.

"'Lionel Lincoln' certainly gives spirited battle-pieces — notably the battle of Bunker's Hill, which is a masterpiece." Rhode Island people may care to know that a part of this book was written in Providence, in the home of Mr. John Whipple, which stands on the verge of the old elm trees of College Street. Here, too, Cooper may have studied on the opening scenes of "The Red Rover."

Early spring of 1825 found Fenimore Cooper in Washington, whence he wrote: "I have just witnessed one of the most imposing ceremonies of this government; I allude to the inaugura-

WHIPPLE HOUSE, AT PROVIDENCE, R. I.

tion of the President of the United States." It
was that of John Quincy Adams, who succeeded
James Monroe. Elsewhere one learns that
Cooper had dined at the White House; he gave
a description of Mrs. Monroe as first lady of the
land.

Up to this year the
author had signed his
name " James Cooper ";
then, in remembrance of

PRESIDENT'S HOUSE, 1825.

[119]

his mother's wish, he changed it, and by the April, 1826, act of Legislature the family name became Fenimore Cooper.

During the summer of 1825 Mr. Cooper made one of a party of young men, — which included also the Hon. Mr. Stanley, afterwards Lord Derby, Prime Minister of England, and the Hon. Wortley Montagu, later Lord Wharncliffe, in an excursion to Saratoga and the Lake George country. They went slowly up the Hudson, paid a brief visit to West Point, thence to Catskill, where, like Leatherstocking, they saw "Creation!" — as Natty said, dropping the end of his rod into the water, and sweeping one hand around him in a circle — "all creation, lad." In the hills they saw the two small ponds, and the merry stream crooking and winding through the valley to the rocks; and the "Leap" in its first plunge of two hundred feet: "It's a drop for the old Hudson," added Natty. The Shakers were called upon in their beautiful valley and neat village at Lebanon; good dinners were eaten at friendly tables in Albany; and gay were the times they had in Ballston and Saratoga. Thence to the Lake George region, its wooded heights, islands, crystal lakes, silent shores. For a while they lingered

SUNRISE AT SOUTH MOUNTAIN.

"Creation all creation, lad."

with delight, then turned back for the dark, still caverns in the heart of Glens Fall. These caverns were, Natty said, "Two little holes for us to hide in." He added, "Falls on two sides of

GLEN'S FALL'S CAVERNS.

us, and the river above and below! — it would be worth the trouble to step up on the height of this rock and look at the pervarcity of the water. It falls by no rule at all." Within the shadows and silence of these caverns Mr. Stanley suggested to Cooper that "here was the very scene for a romance," and the author promised his friend that a book should be written in which these caves would play an important part. A story of strong Indian make-up first came then to the author's mind. Before leaving, these caverns and the surrounding country were closely examined for future use.

Besides his youthful and Lake Ontario expe-
riences with Indians, Cooper followed parties of
them from Albany to New York, and several
times to Washington, for the purpose of closely
studying their natures and habits; all authorities in print were consulted. On his return
home the book was begun and rapidly written.
" Planned beneath the summer leaves, on the

GLENS FALL.

far shore of picturesque Hell Gate, above smiling fields and bowering orchards of his Angevine
home, those leaves had scarcely fallen when the
story was told — 'the most uniformly exciting
and powerful of his fictions' — 'The Last of
the Mohicans,' and Natty and Chingachgook
were left in the wilderness beside the rude grave
of Uncas." Again they came into the shadow of
the unbroken forest, as called for by the *one*
friend he now constantly consulted, — his faithful, loving life-mate. At the time of its writing Cooper had a serious illness, during which
his mind was filled with ideas for this book.
Suddenly rousing himself one of these autumn
afternoons, he called for pen and paper, but too
ill to use them, asked Mrs. Cooper, watching

LAKE GEORGE, OR "THE HORICAN."

anxiously by his side, to write for him. Fearing delirium, she wrote, thinking it would relieve him. A page of notes was rapidly dictated, which seemed to his alarmed nurse but the wild fancies of a fevered brain. It proved to be a clear account of a lively struggle between "Magua" and "Chingachgook," and made the twelfth chapter of the book. Why the author called Lake George by another name is thus explained: "Looking over an ancient map, he found that a tribe of Indians the French called *Les Horicans* lived by this beautiful sheet of water, and thinking the English name too commonplace and the Indian name too hard to pronounce, he chose the ' Horican ' as better suiting simple Natty." This book, " The Last of the Mohicans," proved, perhaps, to be the most popular of all his works up to 1826.

A present-day man-of-letters writes of Cooper: "He paints Indians and Indian scenes with a glow of our sunset skies and the crimson of our autumn maples, and makes them alive with brilliant color. Rifles crack, tomahawks gleam, and arrows dart like sunbeams through the air. Indians fleet of foot and full of graceful movement are these dusky Apollo's Uncas. Cooper's readers never yawn over these tales of the forest or the sea. He is the swan on the lake, the eagle in the air, the deer in the wood, and the wind on the sea." So writes Prof. Brander Matthews. That life-student of the American Indian, Francis Parkman, wrote: "It is easy to find fault with 'The Last of the Mohicans,' but it is far from easy to rival or even approach its excellence." It is said that "Magua," of this book, "is the best-drawn Indian in fiction; from scalp-lock to moccasin tingling with life" and the tension of the canoe-chase on the Horican.

During this Lake George excursion a question came up between the Hon. Mr. Stanley, the Hon. Wortley Montagu, and Mr. Cooper as to who was the "Premier Baron of England." Cooper

named Lord Henry William Fitzgerald (3rd son
of James, 1st Duke of Leinster) 22nd Baron de
Ros [b. 1761–d. 1829] as his man; whose title
came from Henry I., to Peter, Lord of Holder-
ness called Ros. Each of his two friends claimed
another as the "Premier Baron of England."
All were so confident that a wager was laid, and
later inquiry proved Cooper right. In due time
the debt was paid with a large gold, silver-filled
seal. On its stone — a chrysoprase — appeared
a baron's coronet and the old Scottish proverb:
" He that will to Cupar maun to Cupar! " The

THE WAGER SEAL.

incident serves to affirm Cooper's wide information and accurate memory.

This winter of 1825–26 Cooper and his family made their home at 345 Greenwich Street, not

William Cullen Bryant

many steps from 92 Hudson Street, where lived the poet William Cullen Bryant, who often went around the corner for a walk with his friend.

General Wilson wrote: " Soon after Bryant went to New York he met Cooper, who, a few days later, said: ' Come and dine with me to-morrow; I live at No. 345 Greenwich Street.' ' Please put that down for me,' said Bryant, ' or I shall forget the place.' ' Can't you remember three-four-five? ' replied Cooper bluntly. Bryant did remember ' three-four-five,' not only for that day, but ever afterward."

During this spring Cooper followed a deputation of Pawnee and Sioux Indians from New York to Washington, in order to make a close study of them for future use. He was much interested in the chiefs' stories of their wild powers, dignity, endurance, grace, cunning wiles, and fierce passions. The great buffalo hunts across the prairies he had never seen; the fights of mounted tribes and the sweeping fires over those boundless plains all claimed his eager interest and sympathy, with the resulting desire to place " these mounted tribes " and their desert plains beyond the Mississippi in another Indian story. One of the chiefs of this party — a very fine specimen of a warrior, a remarkable man in every way — is credited with being the original of " Hard-Heart " of " The Prairie," which an authority gives as Cooper's favorite book. On a knoll, and within the glory of a western sunset, stood Natty, born of the author's mind and heart, as he first appeared in this book. " The aged trapper — a nobly pathetic figure contrasted with the squatter " — looms up, colossal, against the gleaming radiance of departing day; and full well he knows his own leaving for the long-home is not far off — for the remarkable life of wondrous Leatherstocking closes within these pages. Of other characters and the author Prof. Matthews says: "He was above all things a

"Natty, the Trapper."

creator of character. — He can draw women. — The wife of Ishmael Bush, the squatter, mother of seven stalwart sons and sister of a murderous rascal, is an unforgotten portrait, solidly painted by a master." "The Prairie" was begun in the winter of 1826, in the New York, Greenwich-Street home, while Cooper was under the weather from the old fever effects. The closing of his father's estate, and debts contracted against him by those whom he had helped, emptied his purse and left him a poor man. To meet these calls of honor and his own needs, he wrote when not able to do so, and for a short and only time in his life called in the

HENRY CLAY. CHANCELLOR KENT.

aid of coffee for his work. Wine he drank daily at dinner only, and he never smoked.

When Cooper followed the Sioux and Pawnee Indians to Washington, in 1826, Henry Clay, Secretary of State, offered him the appointment of United States Minister to Sweden. It was declined in favor of the consulship to Lyons, France, which latter would allow him more freedom and protect his family in case of foreign troubles. With this trip to Europe in view his family busily studied French and Spanish. Returning to New York, Cooper's club gave him

[131]

THE U. S. S. HUDSON.

a farewell dinner, at which the author said he
intended to write a history of the United States
Navy. At this dinner he was toasted by Chancellor Kent as "the genius which has rendered
our native soil classic ground, and given to our
early history the enchantment of fiction."

May 1 the town house was given up for a
month of hotel life, and on June 1, at eleven
o'clock, Mr. and Mrs. Cooper and their children
boarded the *Hudson* at Whitehall Wharf for
Europe. They left a land-squall — their maid
Abigail — ashore and found some rough weather
ahead before June 30. "A fine clear day
brought in plain sight ninety-seven sail, which

WHITEHALL WHARF, 1826.

had come into the Channel, like ourselves, during the thick weather. The blue waters were
glittering with canvas." A little later Cooper
wrote: "There is a cry of 'Land!' and I must
hasten on deck to revel in the cheerful sight."
The *Hudson* brought up at Cowes, Isle of Wight,
July 2, 1826; "after a passage of thirty-one
days we first put foot in Europe," wrote Cooper.
In this "toy-town" they found rooms at the
"Fountain," where the windows gave them
pretty vistas, and evening brought the first old-
country meal, also the first taste of the famous
Isle-of-Wight butter, which, however, without
salt they thought "tasteless." As eager new-

comers to strange lands, they made several
sight-seeing ventures, among which was enjoyed

KEEP OF CARISBROOK.

the ivy-clad ruin of Carisbrook, the one-time
prison of Charles I. A few days later they
landed on the pier at Southampton, which town
is recorded as being " noted for long passages,
bow-windows, and old maids." Here they found
pleasant lodgings, friends, and a sister of Mrs.
Cooper's whereby time was pleasantly passed by
the family while Cooper went up to London to
see his publishers. On his return they were

HAVRE, BY NIGHT.

soon aboard the *Camilla*, "shorn of one wing"
(one of her two boilers was out of order), and
on their way to France. At midnight they were
on deck for their first sight of France. "Land!
— of ghostly hue in the bright moonlight, and
other lights glittering from the two towers on
the headlands near by." Landing at the small
port of Havre, they had some weary hours of

search before finding shelter in *Hotel d'Angle-
terre.* By a " skirted wonder " of the port their
luggage soon passed the customs next morning
and they were started for Paris. They were
charmed with the dark old sombre, mysterious

WINDMILLS OF MONTMARTRE.

towers and fantastic roofs of Rouen, where
Cooper bought a large traveling carriage, in
which they safely passed the " ugly dragons "
that " thrust out their grinning heads from the
Normandy towns " on the way to the heart of
France. From the windmills of Montmartre
they took in the whole vast capital at a glance.
A short stay was made at a small hotel, where
soon after their arrival they engaged " a gov-
erness for the girls." She proved to be " a

furious royalist," teaching the children that
" Washington was a rebel, Lafayette a monster,
and Louis XVI a martyr." Under the rule of
returned royalists was attempted the exclusion
of even the *name* of Bonaparte from French
history. " My girls,"
Cooper wrote, " have
shown me the history of
France — officially pre-
pared for schools, in
which there is no sort
of allusion to him."
Their next venture was

THE CONVENT ST. MAUR.   HOTEL DE JUMIÈGES.

[137]

Hotel de Jumièges in a small garden, far from the Faubourg St. Germain, where they had an apartment of six rooms. Cooper wrote: " The two lower floors were occupied as a girls' boarding-school; — the reason for dwelling in it, our own daughters were in the school; on the second floor there was nothing but our own apartment." And here, next door to their nun-neighbors of the convent St. Maur, Cooper wrote the last pages of " The Prairie." It was published in the autumn of 1826, by Lea and Carey, of Philadelphia.

Cooper was very fond of walking, and to get a general idea of Paris he and Captain Chauncey — an old messmate and officer in the navy — made the circuit of the city walls, a distance of nineteen miles, in four hours. For two hours the captain had Cooper " a little on his quarter." " By this time," Cooper wrote, " I ranged up abeam," — to find a pinching boot on his friend's foot. Near the finish the mate of this " pinching boot " became " too large," and the captain " fell fairly astern." But without stopping, eating, or drinking, they made the distance in four hours to a minute.

Washington Irving wrote from Madrid the

following spring: " I left Paris before the arrival of Cooper, and regret extremely that I
missed him. I have a great desire to make his
acquaintance, for I am delighted with his novels.
His naval scenes and characters in ' The Pilot '
are admirable." Cooper soon became known in
France by his presence at a dinner given by the
U. S. Minister to Canning then in Paris.

In " Bryant and His Friends " General James
Grant Wilson says: " Scott and Cooper met at
the Princess Galitzin's, in Paris, November,
1826; and, says Scott's diary, ' so the Scotch
and American Lions took the field together.' "
In Miss Cooper's " Pages and Pictures " appears
her father's first interview with the author of
" Waverley," of which Cooper wrote in part:
" Ten days after the arrival of Sir Walter Scott
I ordered a carriage one morning. I had got as
far as the lower flight to the door when another
carriage-steps rattled, and presently a large,
heavy man appeared in the door of the hotel.
He was gray, limped a little, walking with a
cane. We passed on the stairs, bowing. I was
about to enter the carriage when I fancied the
face and form were known to me, and it flashed
on my mind that the visit might be to myself.

The stranger went up the large stone steps, with one hand on the railing and the other on his cane. He was on the first landing as I stopped, and, turning, our eyes met. He asked in French, 'Is it Mr. Cooper that I have the honor to see?' 'I am, sir.' 'Oh, well then, I am Walter Scott.' I ran up, shook the hand he stood holding out to me cordially, and expressed my sense of the honor he was conferring. He told me the Princess Galitzin had been as good as her word and given him my address, — and cutting short ceremony he had driven from his hotel to my lodgings." Realizing all at once that he was speaking French to Cooper's English, he said: "Well, I have been *parlez-vousing* in a way to surprise you. These Frenchmen have my tongue so set to their lingo I have half forgotten my own language,' he continued in English, and accepted my arm up the next flight of stairs." They had some copyright and other talk, and Sir Walter " spoke of his works with frankness and simplicity"; and as to proof-reading, he said he " would as soon see his dinner after a hearty meal " as to read one of his own tales — " when fairly rid of it." When he rose to go Cooper begged he might have the gratifica-

Walter Scott.

Miss Anne Scott.

tion of presenting his wife. Sir Walter good-
naturedly assented. When Mrs. Cooper and
their nephew William Cooper were introduced,
he sat some little time relating in Scotch dialect
some anecdotes. Then his hostess remarked
that the chair he sat in had been twice honored
that day, as General Lafayette had not left it
more than an hour before. Sir Walter was surprised, thinking Lafayette had gone to America
to live, and observed, " He is a great man."
Two days later Sir Walter had Cooper to breakfast, where the Scotch bard appeared in a newly-
bought silk gown, trying " as hard as he could
to make a Frenchman of himself." Among
others present was Miss Anne Scott, who was
her father's traveling companion. " She was in
half mourning, and with her black eyes and jet-
black hair might very well have passed for a
French woman." Of Scott Cooper wrote:
" During the time the conversation was not led
down to business, he manifested a strong pro-
pensity to humor." In naming their common
publisher in Paris " he quaintly termed him,
with a sort of malicious fun, ' our gosling ' (his
name was Goselin), adding that he hoped at
least he ' laid golden eggs.' " Mr. Cooper was

JAMES FENIMORE COOPER. After portrait by Madame de Mirbel, 1830.

warmly interested in aiding Sir Walter's "Waverley" copyrights in America, and concerning their author he later wrote: "In Auld Reckie, and among the right set, warmed, perhaps, by a glass of 'mountain dew,' Sir Walter Scott, in his peculiar way, is one of the pleasantest companions the world holds." About 1830, when Cooper was sitting for his portrait by Madame de Mirbel, that artist — for its pose — asked him to look at the picture of a distinguished statesman. Cooper said: "No, if I must look at any, it shall be at my master," and lifting his eyes higher they rested on a portrait of Sir Walter Scott.

[143]

One of Cooper's steadfast friends exclaimed of him: — " What a love he cherished for superior talents in every ennobling pursuit in life! " This characteristic no doubt led him into that day life of Pierre Jean David d'Angers, whose brave soul had battled its way to artistic recognition. In M. Henry Jouin's " David d'Angers et ses Relations Littéraires," Paris, 1890, appear two letter records of this master-sculptor as to Cooper. In that of David to Victor Pavie, November, 1826, is: " Next week I am to dine with Cooper; I

JAMES FENIMORE COOPER. From a photograph of the bust by David
d'Angers, Paris, 1828.

shall make his bust. If you have not yet read his works, read them, you will find the characters vigorously traced." A note adds that the sculptor kept his word, and this bust of Cooper appeared in the " Salon of 1827." Paris, March 30, 1828, David again writes of Cooper to Victor Pavie: — " Dear friend, in speaking of the sea, I think of ' The Red Rover ' of my good friend Cooper. Have you read it? It interests me much." A note adds: " Without doubt the author had presented his new book to the sculptor," who gave to Cooper this bust, modeled in 1826. Mrs. Cooper thought the bust and the Jarvis portrait of her husband were " perfect likenesses." Later on David's genius again found expression in a bronze medallion of his " good friend Cooper." David has given the striking intellectual of Cooper's head of which an authority of that time wrote: " Nature moulded it in majesty, yet denied it not the gentler graces that should ever adorn greatness."

MRS. JAMES FENIMORE COOPER.
From a photograph of a drawing made in Paris, 1830.

J. Fenimore Cooper

Paris, 1827

"In Paris Cooper's style of living gave his ideas of the duties and position of an American gentleman. In a part of the handsome Hotel de Jumièges he lived, keeping his carriage and service required by a modest establishment; and his doors were always open to every American who had claims on his society. Meanwhile nothing was allowed to break in upon his literary duties, for which a part of each day was set aside." So wrote one who became a friend staunch and true at this time in Paris. Of their meeting he wrote: "I shall never forget the first day I saw Cooper. He was at good old General Lafayette's, in the little apartment of the rue d' Anjou, — the scene of many hallowed memories." Lafayette's kind heart had granted an interview to some Indians by whom a reckless white man was filling his purse in parading through Europe. With winning smile the great, good man told these visitors to return to their home while yet they could. Mr. G. continued: "As I was gazing at this scene I saw a gentleman enter whose appearance called off the General's attention. He was in the prime of life (thirty-five), and of that vigor which air and manly exercise give. I had seen the heads of great men, and there were some close to me, but none with such a full, expansive forehead, such strong features, a mouth firm without harshness, and an eye whose clear gray seemed to read you at a glance while it fears not to let you read him in turn. 'Who is he?' I whispered to a grand-daughter of the General near me. 'Mr. Cooper; do you not know Mr. Cooper? Let me introduce you to him.' 'Cooper,' said I to myself; 'can it be that I am within five paces, and that there, too, are the feeble of the race around which his genius has shed a halo like that of Homer's own heros?'

PROF. GEORGE WASHINGTON GREEN ("MR. G".)

P. J. de Béranger

I was fresh from ' The Mohicans,' and my hand
trembled as it met the cordial grasp of the man
to whom I owed so many pleasing hours.   I
asked about the Indians.   ' They are poor speci-
mens,' said he; ' fourth-rate at best in their own
woods, and ten-times worse for the lives they
are leading here.' "   Later, Mr. G. met the author
in Lafayette's bed-room, and saw how warmly
he was welcomed by the great poet Béranger.
Still later Mr. G. and Cooper met in Florence,
where they had much fine talking and walking
" on calm summer evenings."   Of the Bard-of-
Avon it is noted that Cooper said: " Shakespeare
is my traveling library.   To a novel-writer he
is invaluable.   Publishers will have mottoes for
every chapter; I never yet turned over Shake-

TALLEYRAND.

speare without hitting upon just what I wanted.
I like to take them, whenever I can, from our
own poets. It is a compliment they have a right
to, and I am glad when I can pay it." Concerning the author's habits, this friend concludes:
"When Cooper left his desk he left his pen on
it. He came out into the world to hear and see
what other men were doing. If they wanted
to hear him, there he was, perfectly ready to
express opinions of men or things. It was delightful to hear him talk about his own works,
he did it with such a frank, fresh, manly
feeling."

DUCHESSE DE BERRI. CHARLES X OF FRANCE.

Among the great again was seen the ever-
favored yet not "gai" Talleyrand. Of the incident Cooper noted: "It is etiquette for the
kings of France to dine in public on January 14
and on the monarch's fête-day." Wishing to
see this ceremony, Mr. and Mrs. Cooper were
sent the better of the two permissions granted
for the occasion. Cooper describes the ceremony
— the *entrée* of Charles X: "*Le Roi*, tall, decidedly graceful; the Dauphin to his right, the
Dauphine to his left, and to her right the Duchess
of Berri." Passing Cooper, he continues: "Near
a little gate was an old man in strictly court-
dress. The long white hair that hung down his
face, the *cordon bleu*, the lame foot, and the
unearthly aspect made me suspect the truth, —

[153]

it was M. de Talleyrand as grand chamberlin, to officiate at the dinner of his master "; whereby proving his own words: " It is not enough to be some one, — it is needful to do something." A near Abbé whispered of Talleyrand to Cooper: " But, sir, he is a cat, that always falls on its feet." Yet of Talleyrand another's record is: " But if Charles Maurice was lame of leg — his wit was keener and more nimble than that of any man in Europe." Brushing past the gorgeous state-table to Mrs. Cooper, the author adds: " She laughed, and said ' it was all very magnificent and amusing,' but some one had stolen her shawl! "

Cooper was ever a home-lover. Wherever he might be in foreign lands, he contrived to have his own roof-tree when possible. Therefore, the summer of 1827 sent them from rue St. Maur to the village of St. Ouen, on the banks of the Seine and a league from the gates of Paris. The village itself was not attractive, but pleasant was the home, next to a small château where Madame de Staël lived when her father, M. Necker, was in power. Some twenty-two spacious, well-furnished rooms this summer home had, in which once lived the Prince de Soubise

Cooper's Summer Home, St. Ouen, 1827.

when *grand veneur* of Louis XV, who went there at times to eat his dinner — " in what served us for a drawing-room," Cooper wrote. The beautiful garden of shade-trees, shrubbery, and flowers, within gray walls fourteen feet high, was a blooming paradise; and for it all — horses, cabriolet, grand associations — was paid two hundred dollars per month for the season of five.

" The Red Rover " was written in these three or four summer months in St. Ouen on the Seine, whence the author's letters tell of watching the moving life on the river, the merry washerwomen as they chatter, joke, and splash beneath his terrace; how he tried punting, and left it to " honest Pierre," who never failed to charge him double fare, and of whom he tells a pretty story; how they all enjoyed the village *fêtes*, with whirligigs and flying-horses, whereby the French contrive to make and spend a few *sous* pleasantly. " I enjoy all this greatly," wrote Cooper. Excursions were made, — one to Montmorenci, in plain view of Paris; and the author explains that the Montmorenci claim to being " the first Christian baron " is of the Crusade War-Cry date and origin. His wife

and he took all the pretty drives in their cabriolet, but later he took to the saddle for the out-
of-field paths, where pleasant salutations were
exchanged with kindly-hearted peasants. Of
these rambles Cooper wrote: " One of my rides
is ascending Montmartre by its rear, to the
windmills that night and day are whirling their
rugged arms over the capital of France." Montmartre, he said, gave him a view " like a glimpse
into the pages of history." He often met royalty dashing to and from Paris. The king with
his carriage-and-eight, attended by a dozen
mounted men, made a royal progress truly
magnificent.

Overhanging the river at the garden side
was a broad terrace which ended in a pleasant

COOPER'S TERRACE STUDY, ST. OUEN.

OLD MILL
AT NEWPORT.

summer-house, and here many pages of the
author's next book — " The Red Rover " — were
written. After he left the navy, and while he
was living in Angevine, Cooper became part
owner in a whaling-ship, — *The Union*, of Sag
Harbor. She made trips to different parts of
the coast, and several times, for the pleasure of
it, Cooper played skipper. Under his direction
she once carried him to Newport, with which
he was greatly pleased. He explored the old
ruin there, but no fancy could ever persuade
him to see more than a windmill in it; but the
charm of Newport's situation, harbor, and shore

[158]

THE NEWPORT BOX.

lines lingered in his mind and served him for
the opening and closing scenes of this work.
After its publication he received from some
Newport gentlemen the gift of a little box made
from the keel of the *Endeavor*, Cook's famous
exploring ship, which wound up its world-cir-
cling voyage in Newport harbor. On the lid
of the box was a silver-plate engraving. In
Cooper's story the "Red Rover" appears on
this Newport scene in the height of his career,
— an outlaw in spirit, a corsair in deed. In
early life he was of quick mind, strong will,
with culture and social position, but wildly pas-
sionate and wayward; and smarting under official injustice, in an evil hour he casts his law-

[159]

lessness loose on the storm-tide of life. The voice of an elder sister, who had given something of a mother's deep love and tenderness to the wayward youth, falls upon his ear. Old memories are awakened; home feeling revives; conscience is aroused, and in the very hour of its greatest triumph the proud spirit bows in penitence, — the Rover surrenders his captives. A like change of heart came, through a mutual love of the birds of heaven, to a real pirate who chanced upon a cabin in the forest's solitude and here confessed his life to its inmate, Audubon, who left this " striking incident " a record in his works. However, " Dick Fid, that arrant old foretop man, and his comrade, Negro Sip, are the true lovers of the narrative; — the last, indeed, is a noble creature, a hero under the skin of Congo." " The Red Rover " is all a book of the sea. In Sir Walter Scott's journal, January, 1828, appears: " I have read Cooper's new novel, ' The Red Rover.' The current of it rolls entirely on the ocean. Something too much of nautical language. It is very clever, though." Its author " has often been idly compared to the author of ' Waverley,' but to no such heritage as Scott's was ever Cooper born. Alone he pene-

John Gibson Lockhart

trated the literary wilderness, blazing paths for
those who should come after him there"; — and
a Columbus of letters for others to follow on
the sea's highway was he.

A misprint in Lockhart's "Life of Scott"
made his comment on Cooper most unfortunate
by an "s" added to the word manner. Sir
Walter's journal reads: "This man who has
shown so much genius has a good deal of manner, or want of manner, peculiar to his countrymen." Cooper, hurt to the quick for himself
and his country at being rated "a rude boor
from the bookless wilds," by one he had called
his "sovereign" in past cordial relations, re-
sented this expression in his review of Lock-

hart's work for the *Knickerbocker Magazine*, 1838, and for so doing he was harshly criticised in England. October, 1864, the literary editor of *The Illustrated London News* wrote: "I am almost inclined to agree with Thackeray in liking Hawkeye 'better than any of Scott's lot.' What noble stories those five are in which the hero is described from youth to age!" From "Thackeray in the United States," by General James Grant Wilson, comes: "At an American dinner table" (the talk was of Cooper and his writings) "Thackeray pronounced Leatherstocking the greatest character created in fiction since the Don Quixote of Cervantes"; and he thought the death scene in "The Prairie," where the old trapper said "Here!" surpassing anything he had "met in English literature."

Of Natty's answer to the Spirit Land call Cooper's own words are: "The trapper was placed on a rude seat, which had been made, with studied care, to support his frame in an upright and easy attitude — so as to let the light of the setting sun fall full upon the solemn features. His head was bare, the long, thin locks of gray fluttering lightly in the evening breeze. The

NATTY'S LAST CALL.

first glance of the eye told his former friends that the old man was at length called upon to pay the last tribute of nature. The trapper had remained nearly motionless for an hour. His eyes alone had occasionally opened and shut. When opened, his gaze seemed fastened on the clouds which hung around the western horizon, reflecting the bright colors, and giving form and loveliness to the glorious tints of an American sunset. The hour — the calm beauty of the season — the occasion, all conspired to fill the spectators with solemn awe. Suddenly, while musing on the remarkable position in which he was placed, Middleton felt the hand which he held grasp his own with incredible power, and the old man, supported on either side by his friends, rose upright

[163]

to his feet. For a moment he looked about him, as if to invite all in presence to listen (the lingering remnant of human frailty), and then, with a fine military elevation of the head, and with a voice that might be heard in every part of that numerous assembly, he pronounced the word — 'Here!'

"When Middleton and Hard Heart, each of whom had involuntarily extended a hand to support the form of the old man, turned to him again, they found that the subject of their interest was removed forever beyond the necessity of their care."

Concerning social life Cooper wrote: "Taking into consideration our tastes and my health, the question has been, not how to get into, but how to keep out of, the great world." But for the happy chance of inquiry at the gate of a friend, the author would "have dined with the French Lord-High-Chancellor, without the smallest suspicion of who he was!" Of French women Cooper adds: "The highest style of French beauty is classical. I cannot recall a more lovely picture than the Duchess de —— [this title and blank are said to veil the identity of the Princess Galitzin] in full dress at a carnival ball, where she shone peerless among hundreds of the *élite* of Europe. And yet this woman was a grandmother!"

In a letter dated Paris, November 28, 1826,

THE PRINCESS BARBARA VASSILIEWNA GALITZIN.

written by Mrs. Cooper to her sister, appears of Mr. Cooper: — "They make quite a Lion of him and Princesses write to him and he has invitations from Lords and Ladies. He has so many notes from the Princess Galitzin I should be absolutely jealous were it not that she is a Grandmother. We were at a Soirée there the other evening among Dutchesses, Princesses, Countesses, etc."

Once with and twice without Mrs. Cooper, the author visited La Grange, the country home of General Lafayette, some twenty-seven miles from Paris and near Rosay. He tells us that La Grange means barn, granary, or farm, and that the château came to Lafayette through his wife; that it had some five hundred acres of wood, pasture, meadow, and cultivated land; that the house is of hewn stone, good grayish color, with its five plain, round towers and their high, pyramidal slate roofs making a part of the walls; that the end towers are buried in ivy planted by Charles Fox. He tells how small, irregular windows open beautifully through the thick foliage for the blooming faces of children, in their home-part of La Grange. He gives rare pictures of the great stairway, the General's bed-room, cabinet, and library in the tower-angle overlooking the willow-shaded moat. Beneath this library was the author's own bed-room. Then came the array of drawing-rooms and innumerable other rooms, where hospitality

LA GRANGE, COUNTRY HOME OF LAFAYETTE.

LA GRANGE ARCHWAY ENTRANCE.

seemed to know no limit. Lafayette's cabinet contained many portraits, — one of Madame de Staël, and one of his own father. Of this room, and the library, and his grand old host Cooper wrote: " I passed much of our visit alone with him in these two rooms. No one can be pleasanter in private, and he is full of historical anecdotes that he tells with great simplicity and frequently with great humor." The château stands on three sides of an irregular square, and is one of the most picturesque structures in the country. The winding road enters a thicket of evergreens, crosses a bridge, and passes beneath an arch to the paved court. Together, Cooper and his host had many walks and drives thereabouts, and, all in all, the author fell under the spell of Lafayette's personal charm and his simple integrity of character. Between Lafayette's richness of years and Talleyrand's old age there was a gulf, — one had attained nearly everything worth striving for; the other had lost the same.

Cooper and his family entered France July, 1826, and February, 1828, they thought the time had come to change the scene, and proceeded to England. " I drove around to the rue d'Anjou

HôTEL DESSEIN, CALAIS, FRANCE.

to take my leave of General Lafayette," wrote
Cooper. To Calais they had rain and chill and
darkness most of the way. Passing through the
gate, they drove to the inn immortalized by
Lawrence Sterne and Beau Brummel, where
they found English comfort with French cook-
ing and French taste. One of February's fine
days they left the Hotel Dessein to embark for
England. After a two-hours' run the cliffs of
Dover appeared on each side of that port, —
the nearest to the continent, — making these
chalk cliffs seem, Cooper says, " a magnificent
gateway to a great nation." Leaving the fish-
ing-boats of the French coast, " the lofty can-

vas of countless ships and several Indiamen
rose from the sea," as they shot towards the
English shore, many "bound to that focus of

CLIFFS OF DOVER.

coal-smoke, London." Quietly landing at Dover-
haven, they went to Wright's tavern, where
they missed the French manner, mirrors, and
table-service, but "got in their place a good
deal of solid, unpretending comfort." In due
time Mr. Wright put them and their luggage
into a comfortable post-coach, and on the road
he called "quite rotten, sir," to London. To
Americans, at that date, the road proved good,
and also the horses that made the sixteen miles
to Canterbury in an hour and a half, where

CANTERBURY CATHEDRAL CHOIR.

they drove to another Mr. Wright's; going to four of the name between Dover and London, Cooper concluded with an apology that " it was literally all Wright on this road." The visit to Canterbury cathedral was made during " morning vespers in the choir. It sounded odd to hear our own beautiful service in our own tongue, in such a place, after the *Latin* chants of canons; and we stood listening with reverence without the screen." London met them " several miles in the suburbs down the river,"

[171]

GREEN GATE, CANTERBURY.

but they suddenly burst out onto Waterloo
bridge, over which they were whirled into the
Strand and set down at Wright's hotel, Adam
Street, Adelphi; " and," wrote Cooper, " we were
soon refreshing ourselves with some of worthy
Mrs. Wright's excellent tea."

The second night in London Cooper, stretched
out on a sofa, was reading, when some street
musicians began to play beneath his window several tunes without success; " finally," he wrote,
" the rogues contrived, after all, to abstract half
a crown from my pocket by suddenly striking
up ' Yankee Doodle!' " After some hunting
they took a small house in St. James Place,
which gave them " a tiny drawing-room, a dining-room, three bed-rooms, offices, and house-

ST. JAMES PLACE, LONDON.

service for a guinea per day." A guinea more
weekly was added for their three fires, and their
own maid and man gave personal service during
this London season. Of his man-servant Cooper
wrote: "The English footman I engaged is a
steady, little, old man, with a red face and a
powdered poll, who appears in black breeches
and coat, but who says himself that his size has
marred his fortune. He is cockney born, about
fifty; quality and splendor act forcibly on his
imagination, and he is much condemned in the
houses where I visit on account of his dwarfish
stature"; and we are told that the English
favor pretty faces for their maids and fine figures for their footmen.

[173]

To a Mr. Spencer whom Cooper met in France was due the visit soon paid him by his near neighbor, the author of the " Pleasures of Mem-

SIR FRANCIS CHANTREY. SAMUEL ROGERS.

ory." Of Samuel Rogers Cooper wrote: " He very kindly sought me out "; and, " few men have a more pleasant way of saying pleasant things." His visit was followed by an invitation to breakfast the next morning. Cooper continues: " It was but a step from my door, and you may be certain I was punctual." He found the poet's home perfection for a bachelor's needs; only eighteen feet front, but the drawing-room and dining-room were lined with old masters. And in the bow-window stood the " Chantrey Vase," placed by its maker when artist workman

ROGERS' LONDON HOME AND BREAKFAST-ROOM.

in the room where he later dined as Chantrey the sculptor and Rogers' honored guest. The library was filled with valuable books and curiosities in history, literature, and art. Of this poet's dream-home Cooper wrote: " Neither he nor any one else has a right to live in so exquisite a house and expect everybody to hold their tongues about it. Taking the house, the host, the mental treats he dispenses, the company, and the tone, it is not easy to conceive of anything better in their way. Commend me in every respect to the delicious breakfasts of St. James Place!" On one occasion, " Rogers, talking of Washington Irving's ' Columbus,' said, ' in his airy, significant way,' as Moore called it, ' It 's rather long.' Cooper turned round on him and said sharply, ' That 's a short criticism.' " This banker-poet could be severe on his English friends too, as it appears " Lady Holland was always lamenting that she had nothing to do. One day, complaining worse than ever that she did not know ' what to be at,' " said Rogers, " I could not resist recommending her to try a novelty — try and do a little good."

Through Samuel Rogers Cooper was soon

CHARLES ROBERT LESLIE.   SIR JAMES MACKINTOSH.

dining at Holland House, in the much-carved
and gilded room where Sully and embassy
supped in 1603. By a word to the porter, Sir
James Mackintosh had planned a pleasant half-
hour for his American friend in the gardens,

HOLLAND HOUSE, KENSINGTON.

[177]

LIBRARY OF HOLLAND HOUSE.

where was Rogers' seat, and then in the library
on the second floor, where he saw its each-end
tables. The generous space between is said to
have been paced by "Addison when compos-
ing," and his inspiration quickened by kindly
"bottles placed on them for that purpose." The
artist Charles Robert Leslie caught a rare
glimpse on canvas of this library, in which appear his friends Lord and Lady Holland, who
were also the host and hostess of Fenimore
Cooper. We are told by him that the dining-
table was square; that the host had one corner

GILT CHAMBER, HOLLAND HOUSE.

and the hostess the centre; and the American author, "as the stranger, had the honor of a seat next to Lady Holland." When talking, he was offered by her a plate of herring, of which he frankly avowed he "ought to have eaten one, even to the fins and tail"; but little dreaming of their international worth just then, the herring were declined. With good humor his hostess said: "You do not know what you say; they are *Dutch.*" With some vigor of look and tone Cooper repeated — "Dutch!" The reply was: "Yes, Dutch; we can only get them *through an ambassador."* Then Cooper rose to the occasion by replying: "There are too many good things of native production to require a voyage to Holland on my account." Of their host Rogers' record was: "Lord Holland always comes down to breakfast like a man upon whom sudden good fortune had just fallen — his was the smile that spoke the mind at ease." And after his death were found on Lord Holland's dressing-table, and in his handwriting, these lines on himself:

> Nephew of Fox and friend of Gay,
>   Enough my meed of fame
> If those who deighn'd to observe me say
>   I injured neither name.

ROGERS' SEAT.

"Here Rogers sat, and here forever dwell
With me, those Pleasures that he sang so well."

After dining at Lord Grey's Cooper wrote of him: "He on all occasions acted as if he never thought of national differences"; and the author thought him "the man of most character

MRS. JOHN GIBSON LOCKHART.

in his set." We are told that England is the country of the wealthy, and that the king is seldom seen; although the royal start from St. James for Windsor was seen and described as going off "at a slapping pace."

But it was in that dreamland of Rogers' that Cooper's heart found its greatest joy. There

JOANNA BAILLIE. SIR THOMAS LAWRENCE.

he met the artists, — Sir Thomas Lawrence,
handsome and well-mannered; Leslie, mild, caring little for aught save his tastes and affections; and Newton, who " thinks himself " English. Here, dining, he meets again Sir Walter
Scott, his son-in-law and later biographer, Mr.
Lockhart, Sir Walter's daughters, Mrs. Lockhart and Miss Anne Scott. He says Mrs. Lockhart " is just the woman to have success in
Paris, by her sweet, simple manners." He had
a stately chat with Mrs. Siddons, and Sir James
Mackintosh he called " the best talker I have
ever seen; the only man I have yet met in England who appears to have any clear or definite
notions of us." Rare indeed were these flash-

lights of genius that Samuel Rogers charmed to his " feasts of reason and flow of soul."

With Mr. Southby Cooper went to see Coleridge at Highgate, where, he says, " our reception was frank and friendly, the poet coming out to meet us in his morning-gown. I rose to take a nearer view of a little picture, when Mr. Coleridge told me it was by his friend Allston." From the bard of Highgate they went to see Miss Joanna Baillie at Hampstead, and found her " a little, quiet woman, a deeply-seated earnestness about her that bespoke the higher impulses within; no one would have thought her little person contained the elements of a tragedy."

An Amsterdam engagement for early June called Cooper and his family from London be-

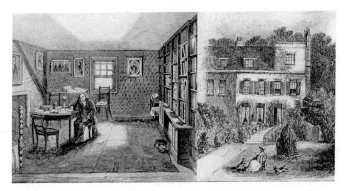

HOUSE OF THE GILLMAN'S, HIGHGATE, LONDON.

fore the end of the season, and prompted him
to say, " The force of things has moved heavier
bodies." Quitting England was by no means
easy, but " the weather was fine and the North
Sea smooth as a dish." They paddled the whole
night long in their " solid good vessel, but slow

BOOM KEY AT ROTTERDAM.

of foot." With morning " a low spit of land
hove in sight, and a tree or a church tower "
rose out of the water, — this was Holland. At
Rotterdam " the boat was soon alongside the
Boom Key." With some fluttering about the
dykes and windmills of Dutchland, a flight
through Belgium soon brought them once more
to Paris.

Cooper was a keen observer and a calm critic
of both home and foreign folk. That he was

stirred to strong words by unpleasing comments on his country appears in his "Notions of Americans: Picked up by a Traveling Bachelor." This book of facts, showing wide and accurate knowledge, was intended to enlighten and clear away mistakes. Instead of this, it drew upon its writer critical fire both at home and abroad, and was the first of the many shadows of his after life. His stories of our new country taught Europe more about America than Europe had ever learned before. His love for, and faith in, his own country were strong. Abroad he was a staunch defender of her free institutions, and foreigners deemed him more proud of his American birth than of his literary birthright of genius; and yet, at home he was voted "an enemy of all that the fathers of the Republic fought for." However, the opinion of those who knew Cooper best was given by his Bread and Cheese Club friend, Dr. John Wakefield Francis, as, — " He was an American inside and out — a thorough patriot." It was said that as an aristocratic American he never presented letters of introduction. Yet in foreign lands his society was sought by the most distinguished men of his time. However of this, the rare pleasure of these London days he ever held in warm remembrance.

Flying from the summer heat of Paris, the family soon left for Switzerland with a team of sturdy Norman horses, a postilion riding the near beast. It slipped and fell, rolled over and caught its rider's leg beneath, but was saved its breaking by the make of his old-fashioned boot, "so with a wry face and a few *sacr-r-r-es*, he limped back to his saddle."

In their salon of the inn at Avallon were curious emblem pictures of different nationalities: one a *belle* of fair hair; another a *belle* of raven locks; a third a *belle* of brown ringlets; — all these for Europe; but for the United States was "a *wench* as black as coal!" So thought Switzerland of us in the days of 1828. One lovely day Cooper "persuaded A. to share" his seat on the carriage-box. Rounding a ruin height "she exclaimed, 'What a beautiful cloud!' In the direction of her finger I saw," wrote Cooper, "a mass that resembled the highest wreath of a cloud; its whiteness greatly surpassed the brilliancy of vapor. I called to the postilion and pointed out the object. '*Mont Blanc*, Monsieur!' It was an inspiration when

seventy miles by an air line from it. This first
view of the hoary Alps always makes a thrilling
moment."

Later came morning rides and evening strolls.

MONT BLANC.

The modest stone country-house which they
took for economy and the author's love of quiet
home-life was *La Lorraine*, and belonged to the
Count de Portales of Neufchâtel. There was
a high field near, where, one day, when Mr.
Cooper was teaching his little son Paul the
"mysteries of flying a kite," they caught the
rare fleeting glimpse of a glittering glacier. *La
Lorraine*, only half a mile from Berne, is noted
as "one of the pretty little retired villas that
dot the landscape," with "the sinuous Aar
glancing between" it and the town. The trim

LA LORRAINE VIEW OF BERNESE ALPS.

little garden and half-ruined fountain were well
shaded by trees, and the adjoining farmhouse
and barn-yard, all Swiss, made a fine playground
for the children's summer holiday. The house
and its furniture they found " faultlessly neat."
There was a near-by common where hoops, rope-
jumping, and kites could be enjoyed. From this
point and the cottage windows " was a very
beautiful view of the Alps — an unfailing source
of delight, especially during the evening hours."
Cooper has given some fine descriptions of their
life in the glow of this Alpine country; of har-
vest-time and mountain gleaners. He tells of a
visit to Hindelbank to see the sculptor Nahl's
wondrous idealism in stone, which represents a
young mother, the pastor's wife, and her babe.

The infant lies in passive innocence on its mother's bosom, while her face is radiant with the light of a holy joy on the resurrection morn. Her hand is slightly raised in reverent greeting of her Redeemer. Of this work Cooper writes: "I take it to be the most sublime production of its kind in the world." And they found it in "one of the very smallest, humblest churches in Europe."

In the small, uncarpeted study of *La Lorraine* a new book was planned and begun. For the story's setting the author's mind turned to the far-away, new home-country, and early frontier life in Connecticut. There he brought the transatlantic Puritan and the North American Indian together — the strong, stern Puritan family affection in close contact with the red-man's

NAHL'S MEMORIAL TO MADAME LANGHAN.

savage cruelty, dignity, and his adoption of a
white child. A fair-haired little girl is torn
from her mother and cared for by a young Indian chief, once a captive in the white settle-

NARRA-MATTAH.

ment. Years pass over the bereaved family,
when an Indian outbreak restores the lost child
to her parents' roof as "Narra-Mattah," the
devoted wife of a Narraganset warrior-chief,
and the young mother of his little son. This
book draws a strong picture of pure family
devotion; even the old grandfather's heart,
beneath his stiff Puritan garb, beats an unforgettable part. Sorrow for the lost child gave
the story its name — "The Wept of Wish-ton-
Wish" (then thought to mean in the Indian
language, "Place of the Whip-poor-will") —

and it has been said to describe the settlement of
the Fenimore family in America.

Many and interesting were their excursions.
One was to Interlachen, with its glimpse of the

CONNECTICUT
EMIGRANTS.

Jungfrau, and the Lauterbrunnen valleys " full
of wonder and delight." At Lauterbrunnen they
walked to the famous Falls of *Staubbach,* which
Cooper describes and explains as meaning " Torrents of Dust."

As the summer had fled autumn winds began
to whistle through the lindens of *La Lorraine,*
and the snow began to fall upon its pretty garden, warning the author to fly south with his
fledglings and their mother before the Alpine

FALL OF THE STAUBBACH.

passes were closed by real winter. Cooper resigned the consulate at Lyons, which was given
him solely " to avoid the appearance of going
over to the enemy " while abroad. A carriage
and two servitors were engaged. One of these,
Caspar, had his soldiering under the first Napoleon, and many were the camp tales he had to
tell in a way to please his employers. At the
old town of Alstetten, with painted wooden
houses at the foot of the Am Stoss, they arrived, more than ready for breakfast, which was
somewhat delayed because, said Cooper, " our
German was by no means classical; and English, Italian, and French were all Hebrew to the
good people of the inn." It was " easy to make

the hostess understand that we *wished* to eat, —
but *what* would we eat? In this crisis I be-
thought me of a long-neglected art, and crowed
like a cock. The shrill strain hardly reached
the ear of the good woman before it was answered by such laughter as none but village
lungs could raise. William — an admirable
mimic — began to cackle like a hen. In due
time we had a broiled fowl, an *omelette*, and
boiled eggs." At another place where they
stopped for mid-day luncheon Cooper writes:
" We asked for a fruit-tart, and — odors and
nosegays! — they gave us one made of onions,
which they thought very good fruit in its way,
and we ate exactly as much as we wished."

" The baths of Pfäffer," he wrote " in my own
unworthy person have wrought a sudden and
wondrous cure "; and of his visit to the Devil's
Bridge over the Reuss: " We entered a gorge
between frightful rocks, where the river was
fretting and struggling to get in before us."
From the yawning mouth of a gloomy cave came
the tinkling bells of pack-horses to Italy by the
St. Gothard. To the roar of the river and the
rushing of winds without they plunged through
this dark " Hole of Uri," which brought them to

THE DEVIL'S BRIDGE.

a rugged rock-rift pass with but a thread of heaven's blue far above them; and here "a slight, narrow bridge of a single arch spanned the gorge with a hardihood that caused one to shudder." Its slender, unrailed, fifteen feet of width was eighty of span, and one hundred above the boiling torrent that fell on broken rocks below, and over it; wrote Cooper: "The wind blew so furiously that I really wished for a rope to hold on by. This was the far-famed Devil's

FERNEY, VOLTAIRE'S LAKE LEMAN HOME.

Bridge; other bridges may have been built by imps, but Beëlzebub himself had a hand in this."

They enjoyed the beauty of Lake Geneva, and were charmed by the attractions of "Ferney," Voltaire's home on Leman's shore, and enjoyed

THE SIMPLON PASS.

the solemn gorge-valley of the Rhone, and
through the Simplon passed into fair Italy. As
they " drew near a small chapel in a rock Cas-
per flourished his whip, calling out the word

FLORENCE, ITALY.

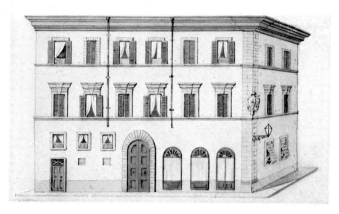

PALAZZO RICASOLI, FLORENCE, ITALY.

' Italia!' I pulled off my hat in reverence,"
wrote the author. Down the steep mountains,
over bridged torrents, past the hill-towns and
valley-lands, they came to the City of the Lily,
— fair Florence of the Arno. " As early as
1829," Cooper thought, " the unification of Italy
was irresistible."

In Florence a home was soon found in the
Palazzo Ricasoli, Via del Cocomero. Lofty of
ceiling — twenty feet — was their apartment, in
which they enjoyed " two noble bed-rooms, several smaller ones, a large drawing-room, dining-
room, baths, a small court and garden within
the iron gates, and all for the modest sum of
sixty dollars per month." The oil burned in

their lamps the home-folk " would be happy to use on their salads." Here, around the cheering glow of great wood-fires, the American author would gather his friends, old and new. From Otsego days a blazing hearth-stone ever rejoiced his cheery nature, and his way of laying the wood and nursing the flames horrified his Italian servants as waste of fuel. The chill of the *tra montana* brought into this circle of warmth and light many eminent foreigners; and of home-country folk, that true American, Horatio Greenough, often basked in the bright glow of the author's wood-fires at Florence.

Later Greenough wrote: " Fenimore Cooper saved me from despair after my return to Italy. He employed me as I wish to be employed; and up to this moment has been a father to me." Greenough's last work was a bust of his illustrious friend, the American novelist, which he proposed to cast in bronze, at his own expense, and place in the field where stands the Old Mill in Newport, and where the opening scene of " The Red Rover " is laid. He took counsel with Cooper's friends as to a monument to the author, and among his papers was found an elaborate design for the work.

Cooper loved to encourage rising talent in young artists. He gave them orders, and also his cheering sympathy. One of these wrote that Cooper gave him a free letter-of-credit on his banker in Paris, and added: " I had occasion to use it more than once, and my drafts were al ways cheerfully accepted. Since then I have paid him, though he never would have asked for the money; nobody but he and I ever knew of the transaction." A Boston man writes of his visit to the Florence studio of Greenough: " My eye fell upon a bust which awakened sea and forest pictures, — the spars of an elegant craft, the lofty figure of a hunter, the dignified bear-

BUST OF JAMES FENIMORE COOPER.
By Horatio Greenough.

ing of a mysterious pilot." It was the bust of Fenimore Cooper. Of the sculptor it was noted that "he always referred with emotion to the gleam of sunshine which encouraged him at this crisis, in the friendship of our late renowned novelist, Cooper."

In the Pitti one day they passed before Raphael's *Madonna del Trono*, and the sculptor pointed out to his companion the fine drawing in the two little angel figures of the fore-ground, in the act of singing. Cooper asked if the subject would not lend itself to sculp-

ture; afterwards one of his daughters copied
the figures, and the result of the mutual interest
in the design was an order from Cooper for a

CHANTING CHERUBS.

group which in a few months Greenough exe-
cuted in marble. It was exhibited in America
under the title of "The Chanting Cherubs."
It was Cooper's "Chanting Cherubs" — the
first group of its kind from an American chisel
— that led to Greenough's order for the statue
of Washington, and inspired the pen of Richard
Henry Dana to write:

> Whence came ye, cherubs? from the moon?
>   Or from some shining star?
> Ye, sure, are sent a blessed boon,
>   From kinder worlds afar;
> For while I look my heart is all delight:
> Earth hath no creatures half so pure and bright.

PITTI PALACE,
FLORENCE, Italy, 1828.

LEOPOLD II,
GRAND DUKE OF TUSCANY.

Later on Greenough came to them " all booted and bearded beyond recognition " save in " his walk and his talk."

During Cooper's later American press troubles his close friend, Greenough, wrote him: " You lose your hold on the American public with rubbing down their skins with brick-bats." And yet, during Greenough's dark days, he said: " What is the use of blowing up bladders for posterity to jump upon for the mere pleasure of hearing them crack? " The author's keen delight in architecture, sculpture, and painting then gave him daily pleasure in the churches, palaces, and art-galleries of *Bella Firenzi*. Familiar from youth with his father's engravings of antique sculpture subjects, he writes of his first glimpses of the originals in the Pitti: " I stood, hat in hand, involuntarily bowing to the circle of marble figures that surrounded me."

Attired in " a black coat, breeches, and vest with steel buttons, lace frills and ruff, a sword and a dress-hat," our author was presented at the brilliant Tuscan Court. Grand Duke Leopold II left on Cooper's mind a strong impression of integrity of character; his simplicity and justice were borne out in his greeting: " They tell me you are the author of many books, but as it has never been my good fortune to meet with them, I can say no more on this subject

COUNT ST. LEU.

than that I have heard them well spoken of by those who have." Cooper was asked "a hundred questions as to America," and assured of the prince's pleasure in seeing him at court and his being in Tuscany. When leaving Florence Cooper paid his parting respects at the Pitti in an hour's pleasant converse, and then presented the Grand Duke with a copy of "The Wept of Wish-ton-Wish," printed in his city of the Arno. Here Cooper and his family had some gay carnival days with their various friends. Among

them was the Count St. Leu, son of Queen
Hortense and King Louis of Holland, and the
author's sometimes host, and "one of the handsomest men of his age" that Cooper ever met.
We are told of the Count: "He lived in good
style, having a fine villa where I dined lately,
and a palace in town." By those nearest him
he was addressed "your Majesty," and held
some "little show" of royalty. Princess Charlotte, his wife, and daughter of Joseph Bonaparte, the author also knew. He met Madame

MOTHER OF NAPOLEON I. MADAME MÈRE.

Mère, who is described as "a slight old lady,
with little remains of beauty except fine black
eyes." She was quiet, simple; in short, motherly,
when seen by Cooper the winter of 1828–29.

Longing for the open country came with the early Italian spring, and a hillside villa just outside the walls of Florence was secured. A narrow lane ran between this villa *St. Illario* and its rustic church of the same name. The villa had two projecting wings with belvederes and roofed terraces, one of which connected with the author's study. Herein he wrote of "the witchery of Italy" — the land he loved next to his own. His letters give glorious glimpses of the Arno, their strolls to Bellosguardo's heights, the churches, monasteries, costumes, and songs of the peasants — all attuned to poesy. Frequent were the exchanges of civility between the author's study and the good old *curato* across the lane. Cooper wrote of him: "The man has some excellent figs, and our cook, having discovered it, lays his trees under contribution." He continues: "One small, green-coated, fresh fig is the precise point of felicity. But the good *curato*, besides his figs, has a pair of uneasy bells in his church-tower that are exactly forty-three feet from my ears, which ring in pairs six or eight times daily. There are matins, noontide, vespers, to say nothing of christenings, weddings, and funerals."

Then follows a rare account of a night funeral service ending beneath his study walls.

During the great Florentine *fête* of St. John,

CHURCH OF ST. ILLARIO AND NARROW LANE.

VILLA, ST. ILLARIO.

the patron saint of the city, — from the Count St. Leu's windows on the Arno, — the author and his family saw the display of gala-boats decked with thousands of colored-paper lan-

CHARIOT RACES, FLORENCE.

terns. They enjoyed the chariot races in the wide Piazza Santa Maria Novella, where the small obelisks point the start and finish of the races. These were followed by the *corso dei barberi* — barbed horse-races without riders — down the longest street of the town. Then followed the French Minister's masked ball, amusing as well as splendid, readers of Cooper's "Italy" will find. But more than all, on their return to Villa St. Illario, were they charmed with the brilliant illumination of the noble cathedral dome, which against the dark skies "looked like a line engraving of fire." So closed this festa of Florence in the grand-ducal days, bright in gay gear and alive with everybody, from prince to *contadini*. Then he came in happy touch with the impulsive, laughing, singing, dark-haired Italians, and to the finer aspects of their nature he was partial. They were in sharp contrast to the Puritan band in the valley of the Connecticut, which his pen pictured in the finishing touches of " The Wept of Wish-ton-Wish," when in his study at *Casa Ricasoli.*

Press censorship and no English printing-house in Florence forced Cooper to leave his family and go to Marseilles. His letters give some pretty pictures which passed his carriage windows on the way. Of Genoa: " The seaward prospect was glorious." The islands " were borrowed by Leonardo," and a circuit of the city

GENOA.

walls was made on horseback. Full of charm and interest was the road "on the margin of the sea" — from Genoa to Nice. In his "Excursions in Italy" appears of Genoa: "I looked back with longing eyes at *Genoa la Superba* and thought it well deserved the title." "The whole of this coast," he wrote, "is as picturesque and glorious as the imagination can picture it." He tells of feluccas and other water-craft that claimed a sailor's eye; and the landward views of Mentone, Santa Monica, the heights, arches, and passes, and the wasp-like Villa Franca, perched on its ledge up two hundred feet — for fear of "the bears" said the guide. In Marseilles an English printer was secured and brought back to Florence. Besides being deaf and dumb his name — Richard Heavysides — bore out the burden of an unfortunate temper to the necessity of sending this printer back to Marseilles. Finally, by the kindness of the grand duke's librarian, a small edition of "The Wept of Wish-ton-Wish" was printed, and early sheets sent to publishers in Paris, London, and Philadelphia. In England the book was called "The Borderers," being based on the story of Eunice Williams of Deerfield, Mass., but it was

more highly valued in England and France than
in America.

The Mediterranean blue on Cooper's journey
to Marseilles allured him into conceiving another sea tale. Its writing, however, was delayed by a mild return of the old fever that was
induced by the summer sun of Italy. Longing,
therefore, for the water breezes, mid-summer
found him within " sight and sound" of the
sea waves. He writes: " July 29 the whole
family went to Leghorn, where the salt air was
grateful, and I snuffed the odor of this delightful sea with a feeling that was ' redolent of joy
and youth.' We feasted our eyes on the picturesque rigs and barks of those poetical waters,
and met several men from the Levant, — an

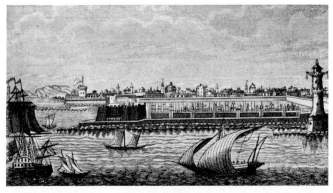

LEGHORN.

[211]

Algerian Rais calmly smoking his chibouque on the deck of his poleacre, many Sardinians, Tuscans, Jews, and three Russians. Rowing under the bows of a Yankee, I found one seated on the windlass playing on the flute, — as cool a piece of impudence as can well be imagined for a Massachusetts man to practice in Italy! The delicious odors of the seaport were inhaled with a delight no language can describe."

At Leghorn Cooper engaged a Genovese felucca, " *La Bella Genovese*, — a craft of thirty tons, beautiful mould, lateen-rigged, carrying two of that sail and a jib, and ten men for her crew." Aboard this small vessel the author and his family spent six days of pure pleasure, yet " somewhat bitten by fleas." They touched at Elba and other islands, and skirted the coasts of Tuscany, the Roman States, and so on to Naples, of which Cooper wrote: " Oh Napoli! glorious, sunny, balmy Napoli!" This cruising along the western coast of Italy in the *Bella Genovese* suggested to the author one of his favorite stories, " Wing-and-Wing," which was published twelve years later. In Naples several weeks were passed at a hotel; thence to a short-time home of their own on the cliffs of Sor-

rento. The very air of Italy was a delight to this sunny-hearted sailor, who so deeply felt the charm of all Italian nature. " The house we have taken," he wrote, " is said to be the one in which Tasso was born. It stands on the brow of the cliffs, within the walls of the town, and in plain sight of every object of interest on the bay. We occupy the principal floor only, though I have taken the entire house. There is a chapel beneath the grand *sala*, and kitchens and offices somewhere in those lower regions. We enter by a porte-cochère into a court which has a well with a handsome marble curb and a flight of broad, marble steps fit for a palace." Seaward several rooms led to the *sala*, fifty feet long, and facing the water. Cooper tells of its tiled floor, gilded

CASA TASSO AT SORRENTO.

couches, chairs, and marble busts. The great charm of the house was its terrace, fifty feet long by twenty-five wide, and protected by a stone balustrade, massive and carved, hanging over the blue Mediterranean, and giving to view Vesuvius, Ischia, and all the coast of glorious sea. Hearing an outcry from his son Paul one day, his father found the boy with his head fast between two of these great spindles — "in a way that frightened me as well as the youngster himself. It was like being imbedded in a rock. Below the terrace runs a narrow beach, where our children delight to play, picking up shells and more than shells, — ancient mosaics. There is a little room off from the terrace I use for writing," and where he could watch the

beauty of the sea. Much of "The Water
Witch" was rapidly written in this study on
the inspiring terrace of *Casa Tasso,* Vesuvius in
sight. Daily excursions were made. When
four-of-the-clock threw the rock shadows far
over the water, they went a-boating. On land
they made " donkey " and " non-donkey " jaunts.
Capo di Monti, overlooking the town landing-
place, was also a favorite resting-place, and gave
some bright pictures of native life. By an
amusing practice of giving their king — a fine
old mendicant with a lame leg — and his daily-
growing train a *grano* a day at the gate, Cooper
and his family on their excursions were freed
from an army of beggars. All were grateful,
and wished the American *admiral* " a thousand

THE TERRACE-STUDY.
[215]

years," — save one poor creature, who blundered into "a hundred," upon which his angered fellows cudgeled him with blows and words into shouting, "A thousand years, and long ones." Donkeys and boats were taken for Amalfi with her convent-crowned cliffs above the sea. Not until the chill *tra montana* and the snow-powdered mountain-tops reminded them that but one fire could be kindled in their vast Sorrento home did they leave it one morning, with ninety-six of their well-wisher beggars in the court to bid them good-speed on their way to the Eternal City.

In the autumn of 1830 Cooper and his family entered Rome through the gate of St. John, and drove across the city to the Hotel de Paris, just below the Pincio and near the *Porta del Popolo*. After dinner, with still an hour of daylight, and eager to see what Rome was like, Cooper called a guide, and, holding Paul by the hand, sallied forth through the narrow, crooking streets over the bridge of the angels to St. Peters. "Pushing aside the door, I found myself in the nave of the noblest temple in which any religious rites were ever celebrated. To me there was no disappointment, and as I stood gazing at the

ST. PETERS, ROME, EXTERIOR.

glorious pile, the tears forced themselves from
my eyes. Even little Paul was oppressed with
the vastness of the place, for he clung close to
my side and kept murmuring, 'What is this?
What is this? Is this a church?' I turned
away impressed with the truth that if ever the

ST. PETERS, INTERIOR.

[217]

hand of man had raised a structure to the Deity in the least worthy of His Majesty, it was this!"

The usual roof-tree was soon found in the

ADAM MICKIEOWICZ.

via Ripetta, where their back windows overlooked the tawny Tiber and gave them views of Castle St. Angelo and St. Peter's dome glorified by each day's setting sun, and here was passed their winter in old Rome. The Eternal City's ruins were most interesting to Cooper; it was his special delight to ride for hours with some friend over the Campagna, lingering among fragments of structures or statues of ancient days. Perhaps none who rode with him gave him more pleasure than the famous Polish poet, Adam Mickieowicz, — a man full of originality, genius, and sadness for the fate of his lost country. All of this won Cooper's sympathy and help in zealous writing and speaking for the suffering Poles; and one, Count Truskalaskie Wuskalaskia, later on found a welcome at Otsego Hall.

Our author also saw something of social Rome, as is noted: He "was at a grand ball — faultless as to taste and style " — given by a prince to a prince near to the royal family of England. Of compatriots he writes: "*We* have had a dinner, too, in honor of Washington, at which *I* had the honor to preside. You will be surprised to hear that we sat down near seventy Yankees in the Eternal City!"

"The Water Witch," now nearly finished, re-

PORTA RIPETTA, WHERE COOPER LIVED IN ROME.

ROMAN FORUM.

quired printing, which some kind Italian friends
nearly brought about in Rome; but the book
contained this sentence: "Rome itself is only
to be traced by fallen temples and buried columns," which gave offense where none was intended and barred the work's issue there. The
story was finished and laid aside until spring,
when, after five delightful months in Rome and
a few days at Tivoli, Cooper and his family
reluctantly drove through the *Porta del Popolo.*
In their own carriage, with four white horses,
and their servitors in another with four brown
ones, they passed up the Adriatic coast to Venice. Miss Cooper's " Pages and Pictures " gives
her father's graphic account of this interesting

PORTA DEL POPOLO.

journey, — how, in a wild mountain-road they
fell in with pilgrims neither way-worn nor solemn, but most willing to talk. They seemed
moving pictures with their staffs, scrip, and scal-
lop-shell capes, returning from Rome. Then

FALLS OF MARMORA AT TERNI.

came Terni and its famous waterfall — a mile
away, they knew, for they walked there. Man-
made were those falls, by the turning of a
pretty stream many hundred years ago. High
bridges and hermit nooks were passed, and
then a long aqueduct with *Gothic* arches, called
Roman in the guide-books; an old temple turned
into a church, and but a trifle larger than a
Yankee corn-crib. Then over the fine road beyond Foligno, and the hill Fiorito, and they
rolled easily down into the Ancona country,
where they found the shrine of Loreto. Ancona gave them their first sight of the Adriatic
— less beautiful in hue than the Mediterranean
blue, it seemed to our
travelers. But with a
sailor's joy in
rope, pitch, and tar,

ANCONA.

LORETO.

Cooper hurried with his usual boyish eagerness
to the port, and with a lively interest examined
its several rusty-looking craft. The next day
found them again on the way, of which he writes:
" Walking ahead of the carriage this morning, we
amused ourselves on the beach, the children
gathering shells on the shores of the Adriatic."
Short stops were made in Bologna and Ferrara,
then northward to the coast. Afloat and a pull
for an hour brought them to Venice. Through
the Grand Canal and under the Rialto they
glided to the opening port beyond. They left
their craft at the *Leone Bianco*, or white lion.
Entering, they found " a large paved hall " a
few steps above the water. From their windows
they could see the gliding gondolas; beyond the

splashing of an oar no sound
came from their movement.
" Everything was strange,"
wrote Cooper. " Though a
sailor and accustomed to
water, I had never seen a
city a-float. It was now evening; but a fine moon shed-
ding its light on the scene
rendered it fairy-like." That

SCALLA MINELLA, VENICE.

[223]

VENICE.

night a friend showed him the other ways than
the water-ways of Venice. Through lane-like,
shop-lined ways, over bridges, and through the
Giant's Clock-tower he passed into the great
square of St. Mark, with "much surprise and
pleasure." By its glittering lamps, and over it all
the moonlight, he felt as if "transported to a
scene in the Arabian Nights." Later he writes:
" I have set up my own gondola and we have been
looking at the sights." For weeks their easy
gondola — which in form and lightness reminded
him so much of the Indian bark-canoe — " went
gliding along the noiseless canals," and Cooper
studied his Venice for a purpose. He became
interested in the details of its singular government and read many books about it. The heart-

PIAZZA SAN MARCO.

less trifling with sacred personal rights in order
to glorify the ruling powers of *San Marco,* as
shown by the life of crime in its secret councils,
seemed terrible to him. And so came about the
thought of writing a book in which both views
of the subject, as clear and just as his pen could
draw them, should be given. And whoever has
read " The Bravo " will know that it faithfully
pictures Venetian life. The great Piazza, the
splendid church, the towering belfry, — rebuilt,
— the small Piazza and its columns; the Palace
of the Doge, with its court, well, giant's stairway, lions' mouths, dungeons and roof prisons,
and the Bridge-of-Sighs, leading to its neighbor,

PALACE OF THE DOGE.

the Prison Building — all are here, with beautiful *Venetia* in the pride of her most glorious
days near their waning. These and much more
make up the fearful picture of Venice's cold
cruelty, as revealed to the author of " The
Bravo " in authentic historical records. Gelsomina, the jailer's daughter, a sweet and deli-
cately-drawn character, got her name and general character from real life. Miss Cooper
writes that when their " family was living on
the cliffs of Sorrento a young peasant girl became one of the household, — half nurse, half
playfellow to the children. She bore the sweet
name of Gelsomina. Simple, innocent, and
childlike, yet faithful to duty, Gelsomina was

TASSO'S WELL.

soon in high favor with great and small, and, in
charge of the young flock, made one of every
family party about the bay." At such times
" she was always in gay costume, — light-blue
silk jacket with gold lace; a flowing skirt; her
dark hair well garnished with long golden pins
and bodkins; a gold chain of manifold strands
encircled her throat, and drops long and heavy
hung from her ears. One afternoon, after playing with her young charges, Gelsomina went for
water to that picturesque marble well in the
court. While bending over the curbstone and
drawing up the bucket, like Zara-of-Moriah
fame, she dropped one of her long, heavy ear-
rings into the water. Great was the lamenta-

tion of the simple creature! Warm was the sympathy of the household." But the old well was far too deep to give up this heirloom and family treasure, which was gone beyond Gelsomina's tears to recover. Gelsomina would have followed her American friends north, but a portly, stately, dignified aunt "would not trust her so far from the orange-groves of Sorrento." When the hour of parting came, pretty Gelsomina received from her mistress a fine pair of new ear-rings, and tears of gratitude fell upon the trinkets as she kissed the hand of the giver. Her name and something of her sweet innocence and fidelity were given to the jailer's daughter of "The Bravo."

> "The well is deep — far down they lie,
>   beneath the cold, blue water!
> My ear-rings! my ear-rings!"

This book, one of Cooper's favorite works, was an artist's picture of Venice, and was written to martial music in Paris, in 1830, where Cooper arrived on the eve of a revolution, for a stay of three years. It was published by Lea and Carey, Philadelphia, in 1834, and did not find favor in America, but was much liked in Germany and

THE BRAVO.

France. Prof. Brander Matthews writes: —
" The scene in which Antonio, the old fisherman,
is shrived by the Carmelite monk, in his boat,
under the midnight moon upon the lagoon, is one
of the finest in the whole range of literature in
fiction."

Concerning the carrying off of the art treasures of Venice by the French, Cooper wrote:
" One great picture escaped them; it stood in
a dark chapel completely covered with dust and
smoke. Within a few years some artist had the
curiosity to examine this then unknown altar-
piece. The picture was taken down, and being
thoroughly cleaned, proved to be ' The Assumption ' " — Titian's masterpiece, some think. It is
now in the Academy of Fine Arts in Venice.

[229]

GLORY OF THE ASSUMPTION.
ABSOLUTION OF ANTONIO.

Cooper tells of a monument Canova had "designed for Titian, beautifully chiseled out of spotless marble." The author found it "beneath the gloomy arches of the church," and thought it "singularly dramatic and startling"; but it had been erected to the honor of Canova himself instead of to the painter!

From Venice Cooper and family went by way of Tyrol to Munich, where he much admired the king of Bavaria's art collections. After this brief visit they moved on to Dresden, passing here some pleasant months in a cheerful apartment overlooking the Alt Market. The quaint and busy show of homely German life, the town, gardens, river, bridge, and fine gallery

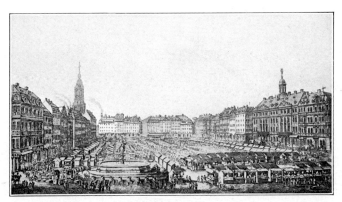

ALT MARKET, DRESDEN.

"worthy of Italy," were enjoyed. *The Water Witch*, "wrecked on the Tiber, was now safely launched on the broader waters of the Elbe." It was issued by Lea and Carey, Philadelphia, in 1830.

Comparing national traits became at times an unfortunate habit with Cooper. He was provoked by a Dresden schoolmaster's surprise that his children were not black; and, again, because he could not convince an English scholar that in Boston " to gouge " did not mean the cruel practice " to squeeze out a man's eyes with the thumb." This English scholar was Sir James Mackintosh.

On the return to Paris from Germany several places were tried before finding a short distance across the Seine, No. 59 rue St. Dominique, — an off-and-on home for three years. Here the salon was thirty feet long and lofty — to a sailor's delight, seventeen feet; above the doors were paintings in gilded frames; and there were four large mirrors, and vast windows reaching to the floor. The dining-room, even larger, opened on the garden. After this manner the doctor of the Duke of Orleans built his home for himself — and this American tenant.

The turmoil in this city of light at once attracted him in the near view of the Revolution of July. Having known General Lafayette since 1824, these two fine men were brought in close touch on Cooper's second visit to Paris. In 1831 the Marquis Lafayette was the center of American life here, and consequently he and our author were constantly and intimately thrown together.

Lafayette's neat, simple apartment in a hotel of some pretension was in the rue d'Anjou. There were a large antechamber, two salons, and an inner room, where he wrote, and finally had his bed. His town servants were his German valet, Bastien, who served during the last visit to America, a footman, and a coachman. Cooper wrote: " When I show myself at the door Bastien makes a signal of

LAFAYETTE'S RUE D'ANJOU HOME, PARIS.

assent, intimates that the general is at dinner;
but I am at once ushered into the bed-room.
Here I find Lafayette at table — so small as to

GENERAL LAFAYETTE'S BED-ROOM.

be covered with a napkin, his little white dog his
only companion." It was understood that the
guest had dined, so he takes a seat in the chimney-
corner, and as they talk the dinner goes on to its
finish of dates, which are shared by the visitor.
The last of these pleasant visits grew from the
usual half hour to almost two, as they chatted of
the great and small and all in their fine way. Lafayette thought Louis Philippe " the falsest
man " he ever met. Of Charles X he " spoke
kindly," giving him " an exactly opposite character," and Marie Antoinette he believed " an
injured woman."

[234]

When Mr. McLane, our minister to England, made a flight to Paris in 1830, Lafayette
strongly urged Cooper to give him the pleasure

QUEEN MARIE AMÉLIE.

of presenting him with Mr. McLane to Louis Philippe at a Palais Royal "evening." Concerning the event Cooper noted: "Though such a visit was contrary to my quiet habits, I could do nothing but comply." His book on France relates the event and concludes with: "We all got invitations to dine at the palace in a day or two." But Cooper "never had any faith in the republican king," and thought "General Lafayette had been the dupe of his own good faith and kind feelings." Queen Marie Amélie, who was the daughter of Ferdinand I of the two Sicilies, asked Cooper which he most preferred of all the lands he had visited. His quick and strictly truthful reply was: "That in which your majesty was born for its nature, and that in which your majesty reigns for its society." As the "evening " was for men Cooper noticed that " the queen and her ladies wore bonnets."

December 8, 1830 the Americans in Paris gave General Lafayette a dinner over which Cooper presided. And, says Professor Lounsbury, " in a speech of marked fervor and ability, he had dwelt upon the debt due from the United States to the gallant Frenchman, who had ventured fortune and life to aid a nation struggling against great odds to be free." As " It was not in his [Cooper's] nature to have his deeds give lie to his words," he was fairly caught in a public controversy that brought upon him the following unpleasant results.

During this period a public dispute arose on the comparative expenses of American and French government, which Lafayette was called upon to settle, and he appealed to Cooper as an American authority. In his spirited defense of the gallant Marquis, our author was caught in a maelstrom of harsh criticism. It ended in his victory abroad, but brought upon him uncalled-for comment from the American press for " attacking the authorities of a friendly country " — as that press unjustly termed it.

At Paris in 1831, by the request of an English

friend, Cooper wrote of "The Great Eclipse" which he saw June 16, 1806, at his Cooperstown home. This account was found after his death and appeared in *Putnam's Magazine* of 1869. It included a thrilling tragedy and closed as follows: "I have passed a varied and eventful life — but never have I beheld any spectacle which so plainly manifested the majesty of the Creator, or so forcibly taught the lesson of humility to man as the total eclipse of the sun."

From Paris, in 1832, Cooper wrote: "I care nothing for criticism, but I am not indifferent to slander. If these attacks on my character should be kept up five years after my return to America, I shall resort to the New York courts for protection." Cooper gave the press the full period, then, said Bryant, — himself an editor, — "he put a hook in the nose of this huge monster of the inky pool, dragged him to land, and made him tractable." After these five years had passed Cooper noted, February, 1843: "I have beaten every man I have sued who has not retracted his libels."

In Paris, in 1832, our author was meeting many foreigners of note, and among the Americans was N. P. Willis, then sketching his "Pen-

cillings by the Way," and breakfasting with
Cooper, and strolling with him through the
Tuileries gardens. Samuel F. B. Morse, who

S. F. B. MORSE.

N. P. WILLIS.

was later to chain electricity for future use, was
then a young artist painting in the Louvre, and
helping Cooper to buy pictures. Of one pur-

TUILERIES GARDENS.

chase is noted: " Shortly after the revolution of 1830, passing through the Carousel, he bought a portrait, covered with dust but of apparent rare beauty, from a dealer in antiques, who said it was a Teniers. This painting was shown to Morse

TENIER'S WIFE.
Portrait by Tenier.

and to Archbishop Luscomb of Paris, also an art critic of his day, both of whom verified the dealer's statement. Catalogues and prints of originals of Tenier's wife later proved the picture to be her portrait painted round in form by that artist and afterwards cut to the square.

Some twenty years later Morse wrote: " We were in daily, almost hourly, intercourse during the years 1832–33. I never met a more sincere,

MRS. JAMES FENIMORE COOPER AND HER SON PAUL.   From
a photograph of a painting done at Paris, 1831.

THE CHILDREN OF JAMES FENIMORE COOPER.

warm-hearted, constant friend." Their relations were ever warm and close. Cooper himself was winning, in the heart of France, a welcome for " the beloved *Bas-de-cuir* with *la longe carabine,* — that magic rifle of his that so seldom missed its mark and never got out of repair." Surely his life and pursuits conformed to his motto: " Loyalty to truth at any price." Those who best knew him best loved him. The charm of his family life during these pleasant days has found attractive expression in the portraits of his children drawn about this time by his daughter Susan, as shown on the opposite page.

During the dreadful siege of cholera in Paris, Cooper and his family remained in the stricken city, fearing to fare worse with country discomforts. In contrast to many instances of heroic devotion were artists' funny pictures of the scourge. The Tuileries gardens were deserted, and Paul missed his apple-women friends of the corners between rue St. Dominique and Pont Royal; and the flight through the city of Mr. Van Buren and other friends were a few personal incidents of this awesome time.

July 18 Cooper and his family left Paris for the

Rhine country. They enjoyed Brussels, and old
Antwerp's Dutch art and its beautiful cathedral-
tower that Napoleon thought should be kept under
glass. They found Liège " alive with people " to
greet their arrival at the *Golden Sun,* where they
were mistaken for the expected and almost new
king, Leopold, and his fine-looking brother. Sad
truth brought cold looks and back views among
other shadows of neglect. Cooper noted: The
" *Golden Sun* veiled its face from us; we quit the
great square to seek more humble lodgings at the
Black Eagle, a clean, good house." In Liège were
seen the venerable, interesting churches, which
caused Cooper to think, " I sometimes wish I had

THE ANGELUS.
[244]

been educated a Catholic in order to unite the poetry of religion with its higher principles." He called *The Angelus* "the open prayer of the fields," and wrote of it: "I remember with pleasure the effect produced by the bell of the village church as it sent its warning voice on such occasions across the plains and over the hills, while we were dwellers in French or Italian hamlets."

In the "Life of Samuel F. B. Morse" by Samuel Irenæus Prime appears Cooper's letter from "Spa, July 31, 1832," to

MY DEAR MORSE: I have had a great compliment paid me, Master Samuel, — You must know there is a great painter in Bruxelles of the name of Verboeck-hoven, (which means a *bull and a book baked in an oven!*) who is another Paul Potter. He out does all other men in drawing cattle, — Well, sir, this artist did me the favor to call at Bruxelles with the request that I would let him sketch my face. He came after the horses were ordered, and knowing the difficulty of the task, I thanked him, but was compelled to refuse. On our arrival at Liège, we were told that a messenger from the governor had been to inquire for us, and I began to bethink me of my sins, — however, — it proved Mr. Bull-and-book-baked had come [by dilligence] to Liège (sixty-three miles) and got the governor to give him notice, by means of my passport, when we came. Of course I sat, — the likeness — like all other pictures you have seen of my chameleon

EUGÈNE-JOSEPH VERBOECKHOVEN.

face — has a vastly live-like look, — the compliment
is none the less, and, provided the artist does not mean
to serve me up as a specimen of American wild beasts,
I shall thank him for it. To be followed twelve posts
by a first-rate artist, who is in favor with the King,
is so unusual, that I probed him a little. I found him
well skilled in his art, — his gusto for natural subjects,
strong, — and his favorite among all my books is
"The Prairie," which you know is filled with wild
beasts. Here the secret is out. — He sent me a beautiful pencil sketch of a Belgian hind as a memorial of
our achievement."

Cooper and his family spent some days drinking the waters at Spa, with best effects for Mrs. Cooper — not over-strong since the Paris days. They left its grass of " ghostly green " when the " dog-star raged with all its fury," and " came on old Aix-la-Chapelle, well-cloaked and carriage windows closed." In compliment to the republic of letters the postman called on Cooper here, and like tribute was also paid two posts farther on, where he was asked if he " was the man who wrote books!" That day was well spent when they reached the terrace above the Rhine and got their first view of the towers of Cologne. In " fine, lofty rooms " overlooking a garden, they here enjoyed a night's rest, a breakfast, and then a pilgrimage to " the unfinished cathedral, that wonder of Gothic architecture." A visit was paid to the house in which Rubens was born, it is said, and the very room which sheltered the last moments of Mary of Medicis, wife of Henry IV and mother of Louis XIII of France. Cooper thought it " a better sort of burgher home," and saw it as " a public house."

Again on the wing, they passed the student-town of Bonn, Rhine ruins of charming legend on the near and far banks of the river, until on

an island in the Rhine they found rest and re-
freshment at a convent-inn. The host, wife,
child, cook, and soldiers three, quartered there,
gave them welcome and good cheer. Their par-

PETER PAUL RUBENS AND HIS COLOGNE HOME.

lor was that of the lady abbess, and her bedchamber fell to Mrs. Cooper. " The girls were
put into cells, where girls ought never to be put,"
wrote their father. *He* " sallied forth alone, in
quest of sensation," and got it in the muttering
of thunder, and the flashing of lightning over the
" pitchy darkness of the seven mountains." And
he and the fiercely howling winds from the trees
had a chase through the gloomy cloisters, whence
he saw, in the vast, cavern-like kitchen, the honest
islanders eating with relish his surplus supper.

[248]

As the storm grew in strength Cooper went to the corridor above, leading past their rooms. To-and-fro he paced until a bright flash revealed the far, end door to which he went, opened, and

CONVENT OF NUNNENWORTH.

entered into utter darkness. Taking a few steps he paused — " for the whole seemed filled by a clatter, as of ten thousand bat-wings against glass." His hand rested on something — he knew not what — when by another vivid flash he saw that he was in an open gallery of the convent chapel. The bat-wings were small, broken panes of the high arched windows, rattling in the gale. Yet by the chasing flashes of angry light he saw beneath him grim figures in the shadowy motions of troubled spirits. They wore upon his nerves, until he caught himself shouting: "'Ship ahoy; ship ahoy! What cheer, what cheer?' in a voice as loud as the winds." He was about to speak when his gallery door opened and the withered face of an old crone appeared by a flash; then came thunder, and the face vanished. After a pause the door opened again, and on the same uncomely face, when, without thought, our author gave a loud, deep groan. The door slammed on the time-stricken form, and he was again alone with the storm-demons who now soon grew drowsy and went to sleep, and he himself went to bed, — and, wrote he, "slept like a postillion in a cock-loft, or a midshipman in the middle-watch." But regret came in the morning when Mrs. Cooper told her husband how a poor old soul, frightened by the storm, had stolen into the chapel to pray, where, on hearing strange groans, she dropped her candle and fled in fear to Madam's maid, who gave her bed-shelter for the night. An after-breakfast look at the storm-ridden chapel disclosed other good reasons than the groans for the poor creature's flight. A peace offering made sweet her next night's sleep, when the travelers had gone on their way, diving here and there

into lore and legend of the mighty Rhine-stream.
Near the Prussian frontier was "a castle that
stood beetling on a crag above the road," where
smoke actually arose from a beacon-grate that
thrust itself out "from a far-front tower." Such

attractions were not to be passed, and up the winding way over two hundred feet they went, and over the small drawbridge, guarded by one groom and the Dutch growl of a ferocious mastiff. In walls, towers, queer gap terraces, — giving lovely glimpses of the Rhine, — court, outside stairways of iron, fine old Knights' Hall — its huge fire-place, and its center droplights of lamps fitted into buckhorns — and curious armor, Cooper found additional material for his prolific pen.

During the year 1832 Cooper gave " The Heidenmauer, a Rhine Legend," to the world. While the book itself is full of mediæval, Rhine-country charm, of brilliant charge and counter-charge, of church and state power, unfortunately for its author in its " Introduction " was this sentence: " Each hour, as life advances, am I made to see how capricious and vulgar is the immortality conferred by a newspaper." This brought upon its writer a whirlwind of caustic criticism in the American papers, and soon became a challenge of battle by one who was to prove himself brave, able, fearless, and *right* through coming years of hot and bitter strife. By one of the leading editors the glove was taken up in these words: "The press has built him up; the press shall pull him down." Posterity has forgotten the stirring conflict, but Cooper's books will never fail to fire the heart and brain of every mother's son for all time.

In a skiff, spreading a sprit sail, they crossed the Rhine at Bingen by that postmaster's assurance of "Certainly, as good a ferry as there is in Germany. — *Ja* — *Ja* — we do it often." Through the Duchy of Nassau they tested its wines from Johannesberg to Wiesbaden. Then up the Main to Frankfort, on to Darmstadt, and thence to Heidelberg. It was quite dark when they "crossed the bridge of the Neckar," but "Notwithstanding the obscurity" wrote Cooper, "we got a glimpse of the proud old ruin overhanging the place, looking grand and sombre in the gloom of night." He thought the ruins by daylight "vast, rather than fine" though parts had "the charm of quaintness." The "picturesque tower" was noted, adding "but the finest thing certainly is the view from the garden-terrace above." Below it, unrolls miles of the beautiful Neckar valley country, through which they drove to Ludwigsburg and on to Stuttgart. Beyond,

appeared a distant view of " a noble ruin " crown-
ing a conical eminence. This was the Castle of
Hohenzollern, " the cradle of the House of Bran-
denburg " to which a thunderstorm prevented

HEIDELBERG AND CASTLE.

their intended visit. Returning to a vale of Wür-
temberg they saw " a little rivulet " which began
the mighty Danube stream on its way to the Black
Sea, and drove up to the inn at Tuttlingen, of
which point Cooper wrote: " This is the Black
Forest, — The wood was chiefly of larches,
whence I presume its name." Warned by their
host-postmaster of a long climb of mountain

separating the Rhine and Danube rivers, in a coach and six they left him for Schaffhausen and the Rhine Falls. The mountain crest gave them a sweeping view of Lake Constance when its waters looked " dark and wild " wrote Cooper, adding, " we suddenly plunged down to the banks of the Rhine and found ourselves once more before an inn-door, in Switzerland." So in the late summer of this year their second visit was made to the land of Lake Leman, whose waters are overshadowed by noble mountains; and its surface broad, tranquil, and blue. Enchanting

VEVAY SHORES OF LAKE LEMAN.

distance made a fairy air-castle of a tiny château on a little grassy knoll washed by the lake, but a near view decided the family " to take refuge in a furnished house, *Mon Repose*," in a retired

[255]

corner quite near the shore at Vevay. A boat, with honest John Descloux and his two crooked oars, was soon secured, and many an hour was spent listening to his lore of Leman, as they

FÊTE DES VIGNERONS, 1833.

floated their several hours a day over its waters, under fair skies and foul. During this Switzerland vacation Cooper's fancy was strongly attracted by Vevay's celebration of an old-time festival, *abbaye des Vignerons,* or great holiday of the vine-dressers. It was "a gay and motley scene, blending the harvest-home with a dash of the carnival spirit." Shepherds and shepherdesses in holiday attire and garlands, tripping the measures of rustic song and dance. Aproned gardeners with rake and spade, their sweethearts

NOAH'S ARK, VEVAY, 1833.

with bread-baskets of fruit and flowers, uniting
in the dance *à la ronde,* as they came to a certain
point in the procession; and so went the reapers,
mowers, gleaners, herdsmen, and dairy-maids in
Alpine costume, timing their steps to horn and
cow-bell, and singing the heart-stirring chorus
Ranz des Vachs, or the " Cowherds of the Alps,"
the wild notes coming back in many an Alpine
echo. The festival concluded with a rustic wedding, the bride being dowered down to the broom
and spindle by the lady of the manor. Such a
holiday on the shores of Lake Leman, and the
Pass of St. Bernard, Cooper placed as a background for his plot based on the hard old feudal-
times law — that (in the canton of Berne) the
odious office of executioner or headsman was
made a family inheritance. The efforts of the
unhappy father and mother to save their son from
such a fate make up the pathetic interest of " The
Headsman," issued in 1833. The Hospice of St.

[257]

Bernard so well described in this book was visited by the author the previous year.

When the power to write first dawned on Cooper's mind there came also and grew with it the desire to serve his native land in the field of letters. Love of country and countrymen guided his ardent, generous pen in " The Spy," " The Pioneers," " The Last of the Mohicans," and " The Prairie," written before he went to Europe. European society he entered, and was courted as literary men of reputation are courted there, but always with the honest pride of being an American. Under these pleasant conditions " The Red Rover," " The Traveling Bachelor," " The

The Hospice of St. Bernard.

[258]

Wept of Wish-ton-Wish," and "The Water Witch" were written. But "The Bravo" was followed by such "a series of abuse in the public press" at home that when Cooper returned, November 5, 1833, these onsets greatly surprised him. His nature was roused by attack; but "never was he known to quail," wrote a famous English critic of him, and added: "Cooper writes like a hero!" He believed the public press to be a power for life or death to a nation, and held *personal* rights as sacred; and challenged on these lines he became a lion at bay. Excepting from his fine old personal friends, staunch and true, he had a chilling reception. For saying, at an evening party a few days after landing, that he had been sadly jolted by the bad pavement and was surprised that the town was so poorly lighted, he was seriously warned by these warm friends: "By the shade of Washington! and the memory of Jay! to be more prudent; not a syllable of pavements or a word of lamps could be uttered." Because he thought the bay of Naples of more classic interest than the bay of New York, he was voted "devoid of taste and patriotism." So hurt was he by public distrust that he thought seriously of writing no more; its injustice led him

to criticise harshly many changes which had occurred during his absence. The Indian trail had made way for canal-boats, connecting the ocean with the inland seas; the railroads had come, with other active commercial interests, to stay.

After their return from Europe Cooper and his family passed some winters in New York City — those of 1833–34 and 1835–36 in Bleecker Street near Thompson. There he " first erected his household gods, French gods these, for the house throughout was equipped with furniture from France, and ministered solely by French servitors," writes Doctor Wolfe. But love for

the old Hall on the shores of Otsego grew strong beyond resistance. It was vacant and of forlorn appearance when the author returned to it in 1834. From a simple, roomy, comfortable house it was made over into a picturesque country-seat, from designs, English in style,

OTSEGO HALL AFTER THE RECONSTRUCTION OF 1834.

drawn by Professor Morse, who was at Cooperstown during alterations. Some of these, without thought of the cold Otsego winters — ice and snow on the battlemented roof — made leaks frequent and disturbing. In 1835 Cooper wrote of this home: "The Hall is composite enough, Heaven knows, being a mongrel of the Grecian and Gothic orders; my hall, however, is the admiration of all the mountaineers — nearly fifty feet long, twenty-four wide, and fifteen feet high. I have raised the ceiling three feet, and regret it had not been ten. I have aversion to a room under jurymasts." The library was a well-shaped room of twenty by twenty-four feet, the ceiling twelve feet above. Its deep, dark oak windows opened on the thick shade-trees of the quiet southwest; the walls, well-lined with books of value, could show no complete set of his own. In one corner of this room was a large folding screen on which were pasted print-pictures of places they had visited during their seven years' tour of Europe; a like screen was in the hall. In this library was the author's plain, shining, English walnut writing-table and chair, whose first owner was Richard Fenimore, Cooper's maternal grandfather, of Rancocus, New Jersey; many of

COPY OF COOPER'S GARDEN SEAT

COOPER'S LIBRARY AT OTSEGO HALL.

Cooper's works were written upon it. On the opposite side of the hall was the author's bedchamber. It is interesting to learn from Mr. Keese that the large north bed-rooms, so cold in winter, were known as "Siberia" and "Greenland," while those on the south, and warm in summer, were called "Florida" and "Italy." We are told the grounds were changed by winding walks and the setting out of trees — not a few with Cooper's own hands. And under these fine trees, in their southwest favored corner, shadows and sunlight play hide and seek about a copy of Mr. and Mrs. Cooper's favorite garden seat. Great gates were made for the garden entrance, as heavy and hard to move as those of "The Hutted Knoll" in the author's story of "Wyandotté." It was indeed an attractive home, made more so by its attractive inmates. Concerning these Mr. Keese writes: "Noting Cooper's fondness for animals, the family brought from Paris a magnificent 'tiger' cat weighing fifteen pounds — 'Coquelicot' by name. He lived at the Hall until the day of his death, and occupied the most comfortable chair in the parlor and was rarely disturbed." Finally the old Hall became their only home, and here, in his stronghold at the foot of the Glimmerglass, Cooper kept open house for his friends.

During the summer months he took a lively interest in his garden. From his daughter we learn: "It was his delight to watch the growth of different plants day by day. His hot-beds were of the earliest, and he was the first to grow egg-plant, Brussels sprouts, and other unusual vegetables and fruits." The first and choicest of fruit or vegetable was gathered by himself as a little offering to Mrs. Cooper, and placed by him at her plate at table. And he took great pleasure in carrying with his own hands baskets of choice fruit and vegetables to different friends and neighbors. Many were these that the author and his old shipmate Ned Myers carried about the village to different homes. Many also were the talks that Cooper and his friend and constant companion, Judge Nelson, of the Supreme Court, had on garden affairs, as well as on legal and political questions of the day; many were their visits to the hot-beds and melon hills. "Ah, those muskmelons! Carefully were they watched." This penman was frankly proud of his melons, their early growth and flavor. But

for all his care this melon-pride met its Waterloo one spring in a special box of superior seed,
started in a favored place for light and warmth,

JUDGE NELSON.

and to be early transplanted. Soon the tiny green
blades appeared, duly became leaflets, to the joy
of the Judge and the planter. "Those two venerable heads bending together in close scrutiny
over the young plants was a pleasant sight, in the
author's eager interest and genial sympathy of
the Judge." But alas! neither jurist nor novelist was a botanist, and the triumphantly expected
melon vines basely proved after a few more days
of tender nursing to be the leaves of "that vaga-

bond weed, the wild-cucumber vine." Here too he gathered material for future books, and did much writing. Evening twilight often found him pacing the large hall, his hands behind him, his head doing active duty in decisive nods of *yea* and *nay*, and words spoken aloud for putting on paper in his library next morning. Some of this writing was to his profit and pleasure, and some, alas! to his sad disturbance — as was " A Letter to his Countrymen," published in 1834.

A picture of this Otsego-Hall home life would prove a sorry failure with " Pumpkin " left out. Therefore appears Pumpkin, the family horse, who earned his name by drawing a load of pumpkins for Seraphina, the cow, to eat. It is of note that his horseship carried " a very light whisp of a tail, and had a gait all his own in going at times on three legs and, at times, kicking up both hind ones in a way more amusing than alarming, by leaving an interesting doubt as to fore or aft movement, in the mind of his driver."

Of Cooper's daily active life Mr. Keese notes: " He rose early, did much writing before breakfasting at nine, and afterwards until eleven o'clock. Then Pumpkin, hitched to his yellow buggy, was brought to the door "; and when her health would allow, Mrs. Cooper often went with her husband to their *châlet* farm. Sometimes it was his author-daughter who went with her father; and again, some friend was hailed from the street for the trip. These several active hours would give him a fine appetite for their three o'clock dinner, on his return. " The late afternoon and evening were given to friends at home, or to visiting, and often to his favorite game of chess with Mrs. Cooper."

Some two years after Cooper's return from abroad, a friend about to sail for Europe met him walking leisurely along Broadway with his coat open and a great string of onions in his hand. Seeing several persons turn to look at him, then speak to each other, the friend too turned — " and behold, it was Cooper!" After greetings he raised his bunch of onions and said: " I have turned farmer, but am obliged to come to town now and then, as you see." Kind remembrances were sent to Greenough; and of Italy he added: " There is no place where mere living is such a luxury."

Fenimore Cooper had a keen sense of the ridiculous. His table-talk by his own fireside was full of cheery life, fun, and glowing merriment. "Severe and stern his fine face could be when touching on serious subjects," but his relish of the ludicrous and comical was very strongly marked, and when such came his way in reading, it was carried at once to the family circle and read by him with zest, and a laugh so hearty it brought the tears rolling down his cheeks. While in Europe he outlined a satirical tale in which the men's parts should be seriously assumed by monkeys. An English baronet, Sir John Goldencalf, and a Yankee skipper, Captain Noah Poke, were made to travel together through the different parts of Monkeyland, called Leaphigh, Leaplow, and Leapthrough, representing England, America, and France. This tale was hastily written in his New York home on Bleecker Street near Thompson. Of these countries, their people, and that time, the story was a strong, clever, and ludicrous picture, which in this day would be accepted as such, and be equally helpful and amusing to writers and readers. It was called " The Monikins," and was published in 1835.

Delight in the scenery of Switzerland led Cooper to put in book form his notes on his visits to that small country of many interests and magnificent views. Under the name of "Sketches in Switzerland," it was published in 1836. The France and England part of his "Gleanings in Europe" went to print the next year. Concerning his book on old England, Cooper, in the autumn of 1837, writes: "They tell me it has made a stir in London, where I get abused and read *à la Trollope*. It ought to do them good, but whether it does or not depends upon Divine grace." This effort has been called keen, clever, but untimely, tending rather to set people by their ears than to save them from their sins.

In the summer of 1837 Cooper found himself facing the disputed ownership of "Three-Mile Point" of Lake Otsego. On his return from Europe he found that his townspeople regarded this point — Myrtle Grove — as belonging to them. But Judge Cooper's will left it to all his heirs until 1850, when it was to go to the youngest bearing his name. While willing to allow the villagers picnic privileges, Cooper insisted on his clear title to this pretty shore point; but Cooperstown Solons hotly fought what they called "the arrogant claims of one J. Fenimore Cooper," who, however, finally proved his title

WILD-ROSE POINT OR THREE-MILE POINT.

by winning the case at law. But he lost much
of the good-will of his townsmen, whom he
thought "progressive in killing the red-man and
chopping down trees." The beauty of this Wild-
Rose Point claimed Cooper's earliest love. He
made it the scene where Deerslayer and Chingachgook rescued Wah-ta-Wah. Its flatiron-
shaped pebble-beach jutted out from the lake's
west shore and was covered with fine old forest
trees garlanded with vines; and from their grav
eled rootage there gurgled a limpid spring of
sweet waters. Then a wild brook came brawling
down the hills to find its gentle outlet on the
beach. Azalias and wild roses made its shrubbery, while pitcher-plant, moccasin-flower, gen-

[271]

Cooper's St. Mark's Place
Home, New York City.

tians blue and white, with brilliant lobelias, were among the native blossoms that charmed the author's childhood and made this Three-Mile Point especially dear to him.

The Italian part of Cooper's " Gleanings in Europe " was brought to print in 1838, and later in this year appeared " The American Democrat." Then " Homeward Bound," its sequel, " Home as Found," and the " Chronicles of Cooperstown " — all came in hot haste from the author's modest three-story brick home in St. Mark's Place near Third Avenue in New York City. In these books Cooper told his side of foreign and town troubles, and it was said that not ten places or persons could complain in truth that they had been overlooked.

Thereby New York society and the American press became greatly excited. Cooper was ever a frank friend or an open enemy. A critic wrote of him and this time: "He had the courage to defy the majority and confound the press, from a heavy sense of duty, with ungrateful truths. With his manly, strong sense of right and wrong he had a high regard for courage in men and purity in women, but, with his keen sense of justice, he was not always judicious. Abroad he defended his country with vigor, and was fearless in warning and advising her, when needful, at home. While he never mistook 'her geese for swans,' he was a patriot to the very core of his heart." However, this over-critical writing soon became newspaper gossip, and began for Cooper six long years of tedious lawsuits, finally settled in his favor in 1843. With such able men as Horace Greeley, Park Benjamin, and Thurlow Weed among others in battle-array against him, Cooper closed this strife himself by making a clear, brilliant, and convincing six-hour address before the court during a profound silence. Well may it be said: "It was a good fight he fought and an honorable victory he won" when he silenced the press as to publishing private or personal affairs. His speech was received with bursts of applause, and of his closing argument an eminent lawyer said: "I have heard nothing like it since the days of Emmet." "It was clear, skilful, persuasive, and splendidly eloquent," is another's record. At the Globe Hotel the author wrote his wife the outcome, and added: "I tell you this, my love, because I know it will give you pleasure." In "American Bookmen," by M. A. De Wolfe Howe, it appears that when going to one of his Cooper trials Mr. Weed picked up a new book to shorten the journey. It proved to be "The Two Admirals," and says Weed: "I commenced reading it in the cars, and became so charmed that I took it into the court-room and occupied every interval that my attention could be withdrawn from the trial with its perusal." Mr. Howe adds: "Plaintiff and defendant have rarely faced each other under stranger conditions."

While in the St. Mark's-Place home the family found Frisk, described by Mr. Keese as "a little black mongrel of no breed whatever, rescued from under a butcher's cart in St. Mark's Place, with a fractured leg, and tenderly cared for until recovery. He was taken to Cooperstown,

PARK BENJAMIN.

THURLOW WEED.

HORACE GREELEY.

where he died of old age after the author himself. Mr. Cooper was rarely seen on the street without Frisk."

The shores of Otsego, "the Susquehanna's utmost spring," Cooper made the scenic part of "Home as Found," but high authority asserts the characters to be creatures of the author's fancy, all save one, — "a venerable figure, tall and upright, to be seen for some three-score years moving to and fro over its waters; still ready to give, still ready to serve; still gladly noting all of good; but it was with the feeling that no longer looked for sympathy." It was of "Home as Found" that Morse wrote to Cooper: "I will use the frankness to say I wish you had not written it. But whenever am I to see you?"

The effect of this conflict with the press so cut the sale of Cooper's books that in 1843 he wrote: "I know many of the New York booksellers are afraid to touch my works on account of the press of that righteous and enlightened city." Of these disturbing conditions Balzac's opinion was: "Undoubtedly Cooper's renown is not due to his countrymen nor to the English: he owes it mainly to the ardent appreciation of France."

Cooper's income, from England, suffered on account of an act of Parliament change, in 1838, of the copy-right law. But his London publisher, Bentley, was credited with usually giving the author about $1500 each for his later stories. Report gave him about $5000 each for his prior works.

May 10, 1839, Cooper published his " History of the United States Navy." It was first favored and then severely criticised at home and abroad; but the author was fourteen years in gathering his material, and his close contact with navy officers and familiarity with sea life made him well qualified for the work. He had not yet convinced the press that an author's and editor's right to criticise was mutual; that each might handle the other's public work as roughly as he pleased, but neither might touch on the other's private affairs. However, the " Naval History " sold well and has borne the test of time, and still remains an authority on subjects treated. There are many officers who well remember their delight on first reading those accounts of the battles of long-ago, of which Admiral Du Pont said that any lieutenant " should be ashamed not to know by heart."

One well qualified to judge called Cooper's "Naval History" "one of the noblest tributes ever paid to a noble profession."

When "The Pathfinder" came later from the author's pen critics were startled from the press-estimate of his character by "the novel beauty of that glorious work — I must so call it," said Bryant. Natty's goodness a dangerous gift might prove for popular success, but its appeal to Washington Irving won this record: "They may say what they will of Cooper; the man who wrote this book is not only a great man, but a good man." Balzac held it to be "*un beau livre*," and thought Cooper owed his high place in modern literature to painting of the sea and seamen, and idealizing the magnificent landscapes of America. It was of Cooper and his works that Balzac wrote: "With what amazing power has he painted nature! How all his pages glow with creative fire!"

Concerning Cooper's innate love for his home-country scenery, Dr. Francis gives this incident: "It was a gratifying spectacle to see Cooper with old Colonel Trumbull, the historical painter, discanting on Cole's pencil in delineating American forest-scenery — a theme richest in the world for

JAMES FENIMORE COOPER.
From a daguerreotype by Brady.

Cooper. The venerable Colonel with his patrician dignity, and Cooper with his aristocratic bearing, yet democratic sentiment. Trumbull was one of the many old men I knew who delighted in Cooper's writings, and in conversation dwelt upon his captivating genius."

Personally, Mr. Cooper was a noble type of our race. He was of massive, compact form, a face of strong intelligence and glowing with masculine beauty, in his prime. His portraits, though imposing, by no means do justice to the

impressive and vivacious presence of the man.
This pen picture is by one who knew the author
well.

CHRISTOPHER COLUMBUS.

COLUMBUS' FLEET.

On July 8, of this year, Cooper was made a
member of the Georgia Historical Society, and
the following autumn "Mercedes of Castile"
came from his pen. It relates the first voyage

of Columbus, and " with special knowledge of a seaman, the accuracy of an historian, and with something of the fervor of a poet."

Gleaning Miss Cooper's " Pages and Pictures," one reads, as to " The Deerslayer ": " One pleasant summer evening the author of ' The Pathfinder,' driving along the shady lake shore, was, as usual, singing; not, however, a burst of Burns's ' Scots wha ha' wi' Wallace bled!' or Moore's ' Love's Young Dream,' — his favorites, — but this time a political song of the party opposing his own. Suddenly he paused as a woods' opening revealed to his spirited gray eye an inspiring view of Otsego's poetical waters." When the spell was broken he turned to his beloved daughter and exclaimed: " I must write one more book, dearie, about our little lake!" Another far-seeing look was taken, to people this beautiful scene with the creatures of his fancy, followed by a moment of silence, then cracking his whip, he resumed his song with some careless chat, and drove home. A few days later the first pages of the new book were written. When the touch of Time was frosting his own head, he leads Natty, as a youth, over the first warpath of his hero. And so the " Glimmerglass "

THE GLIMMERGLASS.

and its "Mt. Vision" country grew into the story of "The Deerslayer"; it is "the very soul of the little lake overflowing with youthful freshness and vivid with stirring adventure." On the bosom of its waters is anchored "Muskrat Castle," and over it, to and fro, move the "Ark of Floating Tom" and the Indian canoes, which gave a strange, wild interest to the story. Afloat and ashore come those unlike sisters, — proud Judith, handsome but designing, and simple-hearted Hetty, gentle, innocent, and artless; both so real and feminine, and yet so far removed from their supposed father, the buccaneer. Then comes this Uncas of the eagle air, swooping with lithe movement to his rocky trysting-place. And Uncas is in strong contrast with "The Pathfinder's" "Arrowhead," who was a wonder-sketch of the red-man's treachery

[283]

and vengeance, while his sweet girl-wife, "Dew-of-June," shows, true to life, an Indian woman's unfaltering devotion to her savage lord. Over all its pages broods the commanding spirit of "The Deerslayer," — the forest's young Bayard who has yet to learn what the taking of human life is like. So, in "The Deerslayer," printed in 1841, the "Little Lake" (Otsego), with its picturesque shores, capes, and forest-crowned heights, was made classic soil. Just back of "The Five-Mile Point" — where Deerslayer gave himself up to merciless Indian justice at the Huron Camp, and later was rescued by British regulars — is the rocky gorge, Mohican Glen, through which a purling brook ripples by its stone-rift banks thatched with great clumps of rose and fern. From the gravel-strewn shore of Hutter's Point beyond, the eyes of Leather-stocking first fell upon the Glimmerglass, and impressed by its wonder and beauty he exclaimed: "This is grand! 't is solemn! 't is an edication of itself." Leaning on his rifle and gazing in every direction, he added: "Not a tree disturbed, but everything left to the ordering of the Lord, to live and die, to His designs and laws! This is a sight to warm the heart."

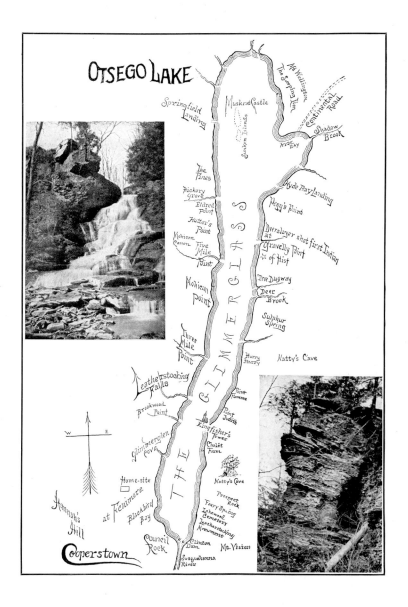

OTSEGO LAKE

Mt. Wellington
The Sleeping Lion
Continental Road
Muskrat Castle
Springfield Landing
Sunken Islands
Shadow Brook
Hyde Bay
Hyde Bay Landing
The Pines
Hickory Grove
Eldred Point
Flutter's Point
Negg's Point
Mohican Canoe
Five Mile Point
Deerslayer shot first Indian at Gravelly Point of Hist
The Dugway
Deer Brook
Mohican Point
Sulphur Spring
Three Mile Point
Hurry Harry
Natty's Cave
Leatherstocking Falls
Point Florence
Brookwood Point
Point Judith
Kingfisher's Tower
Chalet Farm
Glimmerglen Cove
Natty's Cave
Prospect Rock
Home-site at Kenmore
Fairy Spring
Lakewood Cemetery
Leatherstocking Monument
Blackbird Bay
Hannah's Hill
Council Rock
Clinton Dam
Mt. Vision
Cooperstown
Susquehanna River

THE GLIMMERGLASS

The tribes, hunters, and trappers had their "own way of calling things," and "seeing the whole basin, often fringed with pines, would throw back the hills that hung over it," they "got to calling the place the 'Glimmerglass.'" At Gravelly Point opposite, Deerslayer killed his first Indian, and above are the tree-tops where rose the star that timed Hist's meeting with her lover. Some distance to the north is the spot — now known as the "Sunken Islands" — which marks the site of Muskrat Castle, and is near the last resting-place of Hetty Hutter and her mother. And far to the southwest lies a long, low, curving beach jutting sickle-shape into the lake. As a favored haunt of muskrats, it was once called Muskrat Cove, and now Blackbird Bay. Just beyond lies Fenimore, the home of Cooper's early married life.

In the author's pages on England, published in 1837, was expressed a wish to write a story on "the teeming and glorious naval history of that land." Our own country at that time had no fleet, but Cooper's interest in his youthful profession made quite fitting to himself the words of his old shipmate, Ned Myers: "I can say conscientiously that if my life were to be passed over again it would be passed in the navy — God bless the flag!" Out of England's long naval records Cooper made "The Two Admirals," an old-time, attractive story of the evolution of fleets, and the warm friendship between two strong-hearted men in a navy full of such, and at a time before the days of steam. "Cooper's ships live," so says Captain Mahan; and continues: "They are handled as ships then were, and act as ships still would act under the circumstances." This naval historian thought "the water a noble field for the story-teller." "The Two Admirals" first appeared in *Graham's Magazine*, for which Cooper was regularly engaged to write in 1842. On June 16 of this year a decision was rendered in the "Naval History" dispute. One of the questions was whether Cooper's account of the battle of Lake Erie was accurate and fair and did justice to the officers in command, and whether he was right in asserting that Elliott, second in command, whom Perry at first warmly commended and later preferred charges against, did his duty in that action. Cooper maintained that while Perry's victory in 1813 had won for himself, "as all the world knows, deathless glory," injustice had been done to Elliott. Three arbitrators chosen by the parties to the dispute decided that Cooper had fulfilled his duty as an historian; that " the narrative of his battle of Lake Erie was true; that it was impartial"; and that his critics' " review was untrue, not impartial"; and that they " should publish this decision in New York, Washington, and Albany papers." Later Commodore Elliott presented Cooper with a bronze medal for this able and disinterested " defense of his brother-sailor."

Professor Lounsbury's summary of Cooper's " Naval History " is: " It is safe to say, that for the period which it covers it is little likely to be superseded as the standard history of the American navy. Later investigation may show some of the author's assertions to be erroneous. Some of his conclusions may turn out as mistaken as have his prophecies about the use of steam in war vessels. But such defects, assuming that they exist, are more than counterbalanced by advantages which make it a final authority on points that can never again be so fully considered. Many sources of information which were then accessible no longer exist. The men who shared in the scenes described, and who communicated informa-

JESSE D. ELLIOTT'S LAKE ERIE MEDAL.

MEDAL GIVEN TO JAMES FENIMORE COOPER BY JESSE D. ELLIOTT.

tion directly to Cooper, have all passed away. These are losses that can never be replaced, even were it reasonable to expect that the same practical knowledge, the same judicial spirit and the same power of graphic description could be found united again in the same person." Most amusing was Cooper's own story of a disputing man who being told: "Why, that is as plain as two and two make four," replied: "But I dispute that too, for two and two make twenty-two."

Cooper called the Mediterranean, its shores and countries, "a sort of a world apart, that is replete with charms which not only fascinate the beholder, but linger in the memories of the absent like visions of a glorious past." And so his cruise in 1830, in the *Bella Genovese*, entered into the pages of "Wing-and-Wing." The idea was to bring together sailors of all nations — English, French, Italian, and Yankee — on the Mediterranean and aboard a French watercraft of peculiar Italian rig — the lateen sail. These sails spread like the great white wings of birds, and the craft glides among the islands and hovers about every gulf and bay and rocky coast of that beautiful sea. Under her dashing young French captain, Raoul Yvard, *Le Feu*

Follet (Jack-o'-Lantern or fire-fly, as you will) glides like a water-sprite here, there, and everywhere, guided by Cooper's sea phrases, — for which he had an unfailing instinct, — that meant

ISLAND OF ELBA.

something "even to the land-lubber who does not know the lingo." It is said many down-east fishermen never tire of Cooper, but despise many of his followers because of their misuse of sea terms. But more of "Wing-and-Wing": there was lovely Ghita, so sweet and brave, and anxious for her daring young lover Raoul, and stricken by the tragedies that befell her in the wake of Lord Nelson's fleet. The brown mountains of Porta Farrajo, "a small, crowded town with little forts and a wall," Cooper had seen.

ELBA HOME OF NAPOLEON.

He had tested its best inn, *The Four Nations*,
by a good dinner in its dining-room of seven
mirrors and a broken tile floor, and had some
talk with its host as to their late ruler, — he said
Napoleon came that evening, sent at once for
Elba's oldest flag, which was run up on the forts
as a sign of independence. Cooper saw Napoleon's Elba home, — "a low, small house and
two wings, with ten windows in its ninety feet
of front." He also saw the more comfortable

[292]

THE BATTLE OF LAKE ERIE.

one-story home of Napoleon's mother. Other
isles and shores seen then — during his cruise
in the *Bella Genovese* — found place in " Wing-
and-Wing," published in 1842. The knowledge
thus obtained of localities and the Italians led
Cooper to say: " Sooner or later Italy will, in-
evitably, become a single state; this is a result
that I hold to be certain, though the means by
which it is to be effected are still hidden."

During 1843 appeared in *Graham's Magazine*
Cooper's " Life-Sketch of Perry," " The Battle
of Lake Erie," and " The Autobiography of a
Pocket-handkerchief," or " Social Life in New

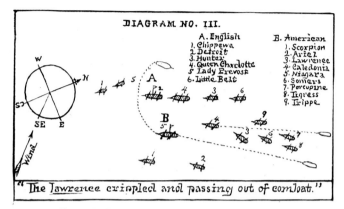

COOPER'S DIAGRAM OF THE BATTLE OF LAKE ERIE.

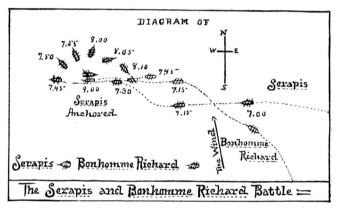

COOPER'S DIAGRAM OF THE BATTLE OF BON HOMME RICHARD AND THE
SERAPIS.

York." This volume of *Graham's Magazine* also included the life of " John Paul Jones," wherein appeared Cooper's masterful description of the

THE BATTLE OF BON HOMME RICHARD AND THE SERAPIS.

celebrated battle of the *Bon Homme Richard* — one of the most remarkable in the brief annals of that time of American naval warfare.

Of John Paul Jones himself Cooper wrote:

" In battle, Paul Jones was brave; in enterprise, hardy and original; in victory, mild and generous; in motives, much disposed to disinterestedness, though ambitious of renown and covetous of distinction; in pecuniary relations, liberal; in his affections, natural and sincere; and in his temper, except in those cases which assailed his reputation, just and forgiving."

Fenimore Cooper was a veritable pioneer in

spirit. He delighted in the details of American "clearing," — from the first opening of the forest to sunlight, by the felling of trees and stump-extractor, to the neat drain and finished stone-wall. On the mountain slope of Otsego's shore, and less than two miles from Cooperstown, lay

STUMP EXTRACTOR.

his small farm belted with woodland, from which he had filched it in true pioneer fashion. Concerning Cooper's "costly contest with the soil," Mr. Keese tells us: "The inspiring beauty of its commanding views caught Cooper's fancy for buying it far more than any meager money returns its two hundred acres could promise." After ten years of devoted care the author is on record as saying with some humor: "for this

year the farm would actually pay expenses."
But full returns came in charming views over
field, wood, and lake, where his fancy built
" Muskrat Castle " and the " Ark of Floating
Tom." Besides, its pork and butter were the
sweetest, its eggs the whitest and freshest; its
new peas and green corn " fit for the pot " were
the first in the country. When the morning
writing hours were over at the Hall, it was to
the Châlet, as he called this farm, that he drove,
to look after his horses, cows, pigs, and chickens.
The dumb creatures soon learned to know and
love him. They would gather about him and fre-

THE CHÂLET FARM.

quently follow him " in a mixed procession often
not a little comical. He had a most kindly feeling
for all domestic animals," and " was partial to
cats as well as dogs; the pet half-breed Angora
often perched on his shoulders while he sat writing in the library." Then there were the workmen to direct, for whom he always had a kindly
word. One of these said: " We never had to
call on him a second time for a bill; he brought
us the check. When I knocked at his library
door it was surprising how quickly I heard the
energetic ' Come in.' When I met him in the
street in winter he often said: ' Well, Thomas,
what are you driving at? ' If work was dull he
would try to think of something to set me about."
Of Cooper's activity was added: " When the
masons were repairing his home, in 1839, he, at
fifty, and then quite stout, went up their steep,
narrow ladder to the topmost scaffold on the
gable end and walked the ridge of the house when
the chimney was on fire." The Châlet brought
to the author's mind " Wyandotte," or " The
Hutted Knoll," a tale of border-life during the
colonial period. A family of that time forces
from the wilderness an affluent frontier home and
settlement for its successors. In " Sassy Dick "

THE ESCAPE — FROM "WYANDOTTE."

the idle and fallen Indian is pathetically por-
trayed: Dick's return to the dignity of Wyandotte, the Indian chief, by reason of the red-
man's fierce instincts, is a pen-picture strong in
contrasts, illustrating how "he never forgot a
favor nor forgave an injury." This story and
that of Ned Myers were published in 1843.

Of these years there are records of Cooper's kindly love for little folk. Miss Caroline A. Foot, a schoolgirl of thirteen and a frequent visitor at Otsego Hall, had always a warm welcome from Mr. Cooper and his family. When she was about to leave her Cooperstown home for another elsewhere, " she made bold to enter his sanctum, carrying her album in her hand and asking him to write a verse or two in the same." Those verses have been treasured many years by that little girl, who became Mrs. George Pomeroy Keese. Two of her treasured verses are:

TO CAROLINE A. FOOT

But now, dear Cally, comes the hour
   When triumph crowns thy will,
Submissive to thy winning power
   I seize the recreant quill:
Indite these lines to bless thy days
And sing my peans in thy praise.

In after life when thou shalt grow
   To womanhood, and learn to feel
The tenderness the aged know
   To guide their children's weal,
Then wilt thou bless with bended knee
Some smiling child as I bless thee.

                J. FENIMORE COOPER.
OTSEGO HALL, August, 1843.

The delight of the winsome little lady was great, not only for the loving sentiment but also for the autograph, which is now both rare and valuable. Not long after the capture of her

Miss Caroline Adriance Foot, Age 13.

verses a copy of them was sent to her friend Julia Bryant, daughter of Mr. Cooper's friend, the poet. Miss Julia wrote at once in reply that she never would be happy until she too had some lines over the same autograph. An immediate request was made of Mr. Cooper at his desk in the old Hall library, and with " dear Cally " by his side, he wrote:

Charming young lady, Miss Julia by name,
Your friend, little Cally, your wishes proclaim;

Read this and you'll soon learn to know it,
I'm not your papa the great lyric poet.

J. FENIMORE COOPER.

On page 155 of "The Cooperstown Centennial" there appears "A new glimpse of Cooper" — caught and kept by yet another little girl who firmly believed the author to be "a genuine lover of children." She writes that to meet him on the street "was always a pleasure. His eye twinkled, his face beamed, and his cane pointed at you with a smile and a greeting of some forthcoming humor. When I happened to be passing the gates of the old Hall, and he and Mrs. Cooper were driving home from his farm, I often ran to open the gate for him, which trifling act he always acknowledged with old-time courtesy. His fine garden joined my father's, and once, being in the vicinity of the fence, he tossed me several muskmelons to catch, which at that time were quite rare." In 1844 Mr. Cooper sent this youthful miss a picture-book, "The Young American's Library." "The Primer" came with a note "written on large paper, with a large seal." It was a reprint from an English copy, and kept for sixty years, it is still thought "delightful reading." In part the accompanying note reads:

"Hall, Cooperstown, April 22, 1844. Mr. Fenimore Cooper begs Miss Alice Worthington will do him the favor to accept the accompanying book (which was written expressly for Princess Alice of Great Britain).

"Mr. Cooper felt quite distressed for Miss Worthington's muff during the late hot weather, and begs to offer her the use of his new ice-house should the muff complain." Miss Alice and her cousin were out walking a very warm April day, with their "precious muffs, which gave him the merry thought about the ice-house." Four years later Miss Worthington received another letter from Mr. Cooper, in acknowledgment of her sending to him a newspaper clipping about one of his books. Of this letter is noted: " His handwriting was fine, beautifully clear, and very distinguished." The note reads:

"OTSEGO HALL, COOPERSTOWN, Feb. 12, 1848.

MY DEAR MISS ALICE WORTHINGTON, — I have received your letter with the most profound sentiments of gratitude. The compliments from the newspapers did not make half the impression that was made by your letter; but the attentions of a young lady of your tender years, to an old man, who is old enough to be her grandfather, are not so easily overlooked. Nor must you mistake the value I attach to the passage cut from the paper, for, even that coming through your little hands is far sweeter than would have been two candy-horns filled with sugar-plums.

I hope that you and I and John will have an opportunity of visiting the blackberry bushes next summer. I now invite you to select your party — of as many little girls, and boys, too, if you can find those you like, to go to my farm. It shall be your party, and the invitations must go out in your name. You can have your school if you like. I shall ask only one guest myself, and that will be John, who knows the road.

With highest consideration,

Your most obliged and humble servant,

J. FENIMORE COOPER.

During 1844 Cooper brought to print "Afloat and Ashore" and "Miles Wallingford" — "which two are one," he wrote, "with a good deal of love in part second for the delight of the ladies." Adventure is plenty, however, and the water-craft very much alive. In England "Miles Wallingford" appeared under the name of its heroine, Lucy Harding; and, says one: "It is a hard task not to fancy he was drawing, in slight particulars at least, the picture of his own wife, and telling the story of his early love." The tale is of the good old times in New York, and land scenes of her river counties.

Those interested in Cooper's review of the naval court-martial of Lieutenant Alexander Slidell Mackenzie, for the execution of Spencer, will find the whole subject and its lesson of fearful retribution in *Graham's Magazine* of 1843–44. Alleged "mutiny on the high seas" was charged to young Spencer. He was the son of Secretary of State John C. Spencer who, as superintendent of public instruction, rejected with harsh, short comment Cooper's "Naval History" offered (unknown to the author) for school use and directed the purchase of Mackenzie's "Life of Perry." Just as Cooper was putting through

LIEUT. ALEXANDER SLIDELL MACKENZIE.

the press his severe criticism of Mackenzie's
version of the Battle of Lake Erie, the *Somers*
returned from her unfortunate cruise. Cooper
instantly stopped his paper at the expense of a
round sum to the printer, saying: "The poor
fellow will have enough to do to escape the
consequences of his own weakness. It is no
time to be hard on him now."

The year 1845 brought from Cooper's pen
"Satanstoe"—quaint, old-fashioned, and the first
of his three anti-rent books. Its hero, a member
of the Littlepage family, writes his own life-story.
From his home on one of the necks of Long-
Island Sound, in Westchester County, he visits
New York City, catches a glimpse of the pleasant

Dutch life in Albany, and with comrades plunges into the wilderness to examine, work, and settle his new, large grant of land at Mooseridge. Professor Lounsbury's able life of Cooper affirms of " Satanstoe ": " It is a picture of colonial life

HELL GATE.

and manners in New York during the eighteenth century, such as can be found drawn nowhere else so truthfully and vividly." The title " Satanstoe " was given in a moment of Cooper's " intense disgust " at the " canting " attempt then made to change the name of the dangerous passage of Hell Gate, East River, to Hurl Gate.

" The Chainbearer," second of the anti-rent series, was published early in 1846, and continues the story of " Satanstoe " in the person of the hero's son, who finds in the squatters on his wilderness inheritance the first working of the disorderly spirit of anti-rent — the burning question of New York at that time. Honest Andries Coejemans and his pretty niece Ursula, the wily Newcome and rude Thousandacres of this story are each strong types of character.

The key to Cooper's own character is expressed in his words: " The most expedient thing in existence is to do right." In the hour of danger to aid in protecting the rights of the people from abuse of these rights by the evil minded among themselves, he held to be the high duty of every honest, generous, and wise citizen. With such sentiments in mind, he wrote " The Redskins " — the third and last of the anti-rent series. Distinguished jurists of our country have declared " remarkable," the legal knowledge and skill in this series of books.

Eighteen hundred and forty-six saw also in book form Cooper's " Lives of Distinguished American Naval Officers," which had already appeared in *Graham's Magazine.* Many of these eminent men had been the author's friends and messmates in early life. In 1847 " The Crater, or Vulcan's Peak — A Tale of the Pacific," came from Cooper's pen. The Introduction states that the book was written from the journal of a distinguished member of the Woolston family of Pennsylvania, who " struggled hard to live more in favor with God than in favor with man," and quotes that warning text of Scripture: " Let him that thinketh he standeth, take heed lest he fall! " and adds, " we have endeavored to imitate the simplicity of Captain Woolston in writing this book." The story of " a ship-wrecked mariner, cast away on a reef not laid down on any chart." This barren spot the castaway makes to bloom as a rose, then brings immigrants to his Pacific Eden, which finally vanishes like a dream. The work is said to be an excellent study of the author's own character.

Full of spirit and vigor at fifty-eight, Mr. Cooper in June, 1847, made a pleasant few weeks' visit to the middle west, going as far as Detroit. The country beyond Seneca Lake — the prairies and fine open groves of Michigan — was new to him. Affluent towns with well-tilled lands between, full of mid-summer promise, where forty years before he had crossed a wilderness, gave added interest to the entire way. He was far more deeply impressed with sublime Niagara than in his earlier years and before he had seen

NIAGARA FALLS.

all the falls of Europe. The idea of weaving its
majesty into an Indian story came to him, but,
alas! was never written. He was pleased with
the growth and promise of Buffalo and Detroit,
was charmed with " the beautiful flowery prairies
and natural groves of Michigan," and wrote of
them: " To get an idea of Prairie Round, — imagine an oval plain of some thirty-thousand acres,
of surprising fertility, without an eminence; a
few small cavities, however, are springs of water
the cattle will drink." In the prairie's center was
a forest island of some six hundred acres " of the
noblest native trees," and in the heart of this

wood was a small round lake a quarter of a mile across. Into this scene Cooper called some creatures of his fancy; among them a bee-hunter, suggested by the following incident.

One morning not long after his return from Europe he was passing, as usual, his leisure hours at the mountain farm. While overlooking his workmen he espied a small skiff leaving an opposite shore-point of the lake and making directly for his own landing. Mr. Cooper thought the boatman was on an errand to himself. Presently the stranger, tin pail in hand, made his appearance and inquired of Cooper and his men whether a large swarm of bees had been seen " somewhere there-abouts." He had lost a fine swarm early in the morning several days before, and had since looked in vain for them; but " a near-by farmer's wife had seen them cross the lake that way." No bees had been seen by the men of Châlet. One of them said, however, " bees had been very plenty about the blossoms for a day or two." The farmer began to look about closely, and from the unusual number of bees coming and going among the flowers on the hill, he felt sure his honey-bees were lodged somewhere near. So, with Mr. Cooper, much interested, the search for the lost swarm began. A young grove skirted the cliffs; above were scattered some full, tall, forest trees, — here and there one charred and lifeless. The farmer seemed very knowing as to bees, and boasted of having one of the largest bee-sheds in the county. Rustic jokes at his expense were made by the workmen. They asked him which of the great tall trees his bees had chosen; they wished to know, for they would like to see him climb it, as Mr. Cooper had said that no axe should fell his forest favorites. The farmer nodded his head and replied that there was no climbing nor chopping for him that day — the weather was too warm; that he intended to call his bees down — that was his fashion. Taking up his pail he began moving among the flowers, and soon found a honey-bee sipping from the cup of a rose-raspberry. He said he knew at once the face of his own bee, " to say nothin' of the critter's talk " — meaning its buzzing of wings. A glass with honey from the tin pail soon captured the bee: uneasy at first, it was soon sipping the sweets. When quite satisfied it was set free, and its flight closely followed by the farmer's eye. Another bee was found on a head of golden-rod; it was served the same way but set free at an opposite point from the first's release; this second flight was also closely noted. Some twelve of the tiny

JUDGE BAZIL HARRISON OF KALAMAZOO, MICHIGAN.
The original of Cooper's " Bee Hunter."

creatures from the clover and daisies were likewise treated, until the general direction of the flight of all was sure. This " hiving the bees " by the air-line they naturally took to their new home proved the farmer to be right, for an old, half-charred oak-stub, some forty feet high and " one limb aloft was their lighting-place, and there they were buzzing about the old blighted bough." The farmer then went to his boat and brought back a new hive and placed it not far from the old oak; he put honey about its tiny doorway and strewed many flowers around it. With the sunset his bees had taken possession of their new home, and by moonlight they were rowed across the lake and placed beside the mother-swarm in the farmer's garden. The author placed this incident in the "Prairie Round" of "The Oak Openings." Its Indian Peter shows how Christian influences in time triumph over revenge — the deadliest passion of the red-man's heart. On New Year's Day, 1848, "The Oak Openings" was begun, and the following spring saw it finished. This note appears in the author's diary: "Saturday, January 1, 1848. Read St. John. No church. Weather very mild, though snow fell in the night. Walking very bad, and I paid no visits outside of the family. Had —— at dinner. A merry evening with the young people. Played chess with my wife. Wrote a little in 'Oak Openings' to begin the year with."

Cooper was a born story-teller, and with a born sailor's love of salt water could not for long keep from spinning tales of the sea. All of which accounts for spirited and original "Jack Tier," which came from his pen in 1848. The story was called at first "Rose Budd" — the name of the young creature who is one of its important characters. But plain, homely, hard-working "Jack," under a sailor's garb, following her commonplace, grasping husband the world over, and finding herself in woman's gear and grief by his side when he made his last voyage of all without her — it is she who had *earned* the real heroine's right to the name "Jack Tier." It is a story of the treacherous reefs off Florida and the deep waters of the Gulf of Mexico.

All those quiet years in Cooperstown the author kept pace in mind and interest with the times, and often gave expression to his opinion on current events. Of General Scott in Mexico he wrote, February 1, 1848: "Has not Scott achieved marvels! The gun-thunders in the valley of the Aztecs were heard in echoes across the Atlantic." Years before this the last chapter of "The Spy" paid tribute to the "bravery of Scott's gallant brigade" in 1814, at Lundy's Lane, not far from Niagara. That Cooper strongly condemned Scott's "General Order" is another record of later years.

Reform — along all lines of service — was Cooper's watchword; his home-cry, first and last, was to "build up our navy!" And, with his knowledge of naval affairs and accurate estimate of seamen of all grades, what an admirable secretary of our navy these qualifications would have made him! His political instincts seemed clear and unerring. April 13, 1850, he thought "Congress a prodigious humbug; Calhoun's attitude another," as was also Webster's answer, which, however, had "capital faults." From almost a seer and a prophet came in 1850 these words: "We are on the eve of great events. Every week knocks a link out of the chain of the Union." This was written to a dear and valued friend of South Carolina, to whom a few months later he further wrote: "The Southerns talk of fighting Uncle Sam, — that long-armed, well-knuckled, hard-fisted old scamp, Uncle Sam." And among the dearest of his life-long friends stood this "Southern" Commodore, William Branford Shubrick. Yet in close quarters, "he would rather have died than lied to him." His standards of honesty were as rock-hewn; and his words on his friend Lawrence perhaps apply as aptly to himself: "There was no more dodge in him than there was in the mainmast."

HON. GERRIT SMITH.

During some years prior to 1850, political party issues on " Anti-slavery," grew from mild to violent. And famous in the annals of Cooperstown was the spirited debate, between Mr. Cooper, for colonization, and his friend, the Hon. Gerrit Smith, for immediate abolition. This vital question of national interest was given able and exhaustive treatment by both debators who spoke several hours while " The audience listened with riveted attention." At its close the two gentlemen walked arm in arm to the " Hall," Cooper's home, where they dined together.

From Mr. Keese comes an anecdote of Commodore Shubrick's visit to his old shipmate at Cooperstown: " Mr. Cooper had a raw Irishman in his employ, as a man of all work. Sending him to the post-office one day for the mail, he told him to ask if there were any letters for Commodore Shubrick. Pat came to the window and with great confidence called out, ' Is there any letter for Commodore Brickbat? ' ' Who? ' said the astonished postmaster. The name was repeated. A villager coming in at that time, the postmaster asked him if he knew who was visiting Mr. Cooper. ' Commodore Shubrick,' was the reply. ' Ah, that 's the name!' said Pat; ' and sure, did n't I come near it, though!' "

Possibly the sailing of Sir John Franklin in 1845 for the frozen country of the North Star led Fenimore Cooper to write " The Sea Lions," in the winter of 1849. When the Highlands were white, and its tree-life hoary with frost, the author could pen best his picture of a voyage to the ice-bergs, rifts, and snow-drifts, for which his two schooners, both called *The Sea Lion*, were launched.

In the early years of his married life Cooper made many visits to the island home of a relative, by marriage, who, off the eastern shore of Long Island, led a half-sea life that was full

of attraction for the young sailor. This gentleman only, his family and dependents, lived on
Shelter Island, between which and the mainland
all coming and going was by boat. Here they
had shooting, fishing, and cruising a-plenty.
The author's thorough knowledge of these
waters was the probable reason for starting his
two sealers from this port in search of valuable sealing-grounds in the polar seas. The
schooners and their captains were American.
One of the sealers was owned by an old, hard-
fisted miser of Puritanic pattern, whose sweet
niece Mary, pretty and simply good, makes the

[319]

very lovable heroine of this book. Beneath the low porch and within the thrifty garden and great orchard of her island home, Mary's heart had been captured by Roswell Gardner, the daring young captain of her uncle's schooner *The Sea Lion*. In the faith of the Star and the Cross the young girl worshipped with strong and childlike piety, while her lover " stood coldly by and erect with covered head," — a doubter, but honestly striving to find his balance. Mary prays and hopes while the young man sails to the far-away ice land, where, shipwrecked and alone with his Maker, he finds the light of Truth shining for him on the far-away shores of his frozen hold. Of this sea tale Professor Lounsbury writes: " ' The Sea Lions ' is certainly one of the most remarkable conceptions that it ever entered into the mind of a novelist to create." And he adds: " It is a powerful story."

" Ways of the Hour " came from Cooper's pen in 1850. The purpose of this story was to attack trial by jury.

From the time of Cooper's friendship with Charles Mathews in the early 1820's, he had been in touch with the stage, and in June, 1850,

CHARLES MATHEWS.　　　JAMES H. HACKETT.

he mentions writing a three-act play in " ridi-
cule of new notions." The title was " Upside
Down; or, Philosophy in Petticoats " — a comedy. Of this play Cooper's friend Hackett, the
American Falstaff of that day, wrote him: " I
was at Burton's its first night and saw the whole
of the play. The first act told well; the second,
pretty well, but grew heavy; the third dragged
until the conclusion surprised the attention into
warm applause."

This clever but not over-successful farce
closed the literary career of James Fenimore
Cooper.

Of Charles Mathews, the peerless comedy artist of England, and Fenimore Cooper, his old-time friend, Dr. John Wakefield Francis wrote:

"During a memorable excursion made to Albany with [the actor] Dunlap, Mathews, and Mr. Cooper in the spring of 1823, I found him abounding in dramatic anecdotes as well as associations the striking scenery of the Hudson brought to mind. 'The Spy' was, however, the leading subject of Mathews' conversation. Cooper unfolded his intention of writing a series of works illustrative of his country, revolutionary occurrences, and the red man of the western world. Mathews expressed in strong terms the patriotic benefits of such an undertaking, and complimented Cooper on the specimen already furnished in Harvey Birch. The approbation of Mathews could never be slightly appreciated. There was little of flattery in him at any time. He was a sort of 'My Lord Lofty,' who valued himself in pride of opinion. Such an individual could not but enlist the feelings of Mr. Cooper. I hardly know whether I have ever seen Mr. Cooper manifest as much enthusiasm with any other person when occasion was felicitous, the subject of interest, and the comedian in his happy vein. Dunlap, were he speaking, might tell you of his [Cooper's] gratuities to the unfortunate playwright and the dramatic performer." In 1832 William Dunlap's "History of the American Theatre" was "Dedicated to James Fenimore Cooper Esq., by his Friend, the Author."

It was in this year of 1850 that the author's daughter, Susan Augusta, had her "Rural Hours" about ready to print. And of this book her father wrote: "It will be out in July. There is elegance, purity, knowledge, and grace about it. It will make her *the* Cooper at once. Quite puts her papa's nose out of joint." More, concerning this book and New York City of that day, appears in her father's letter to her mother, written in that city at the Broadway Hotel, September 19, 1850.

BROADWAY HOTEL, September 19, 1850.

MY BELOVED S, — The post office is sadly out of joint. I wrote you the day I arrived . . . Right and left I hear of "Rural Hours." I am stopped in the street a dozen times a day to congratulate me. The price of the fine edition is $7.00. It will be the presentation volume of the season. I can see that Putnam expects to sell some eight hundred or a thousand of them. . . The improvements here are wonderful. They build chiefly of brown freestone and noble edifices of five and six stories with a good deal of architectural pretension . . . I sat three times for lithographs yesterday and with vastly better success than before. The pictures are all very like and very pleasing. I am to have one which will fall to your lot as a matter of course. Your letter of Tuesday reached me this morning. You ought to have had three letters from me by Tuesday evening. F.'s [the author's daughter Frances] shawl went by " A." I suppose it is a courting shawl. It is almost the only one of the kind Stewart had — a little too grave perhaps but scarcely so for the country. Stewart is making a palace of a store. He takes the whole front of the block on Broadway with fifteen windows in front — and all of marble. With the tenderest regards to all, I remain yours

Most affectionately,　　J. F. C.

Miss Cooper makes alive each season's charms, as they pass over the Glimmerglass and wane be-

STEWART'S MARBLE PALACE.

MISS SUSAN AUGUSTA COOPER ABOUT 1850.

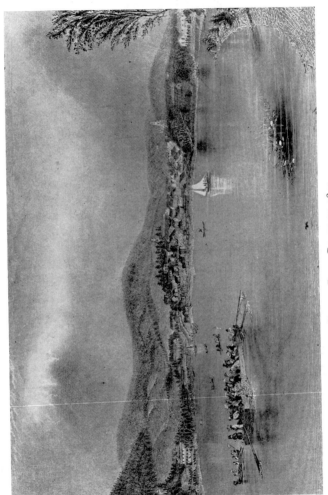

OTSEGO LAKE PARTY IN 1840.

yond Hannah's Hill. From gentry to humble-
folk, real Cooperstown types appear and disap-
pear among these pages; and even the "half-a-
dozen stores" have place, where "at the same
counter you may buy kid gloves and a spade; a
lace veil and a jug of molasses; a satin dress and
a broom," among other things of even greater
variety. She tells how St. Valentine's Day was
celebrated in a very original way as *Vrouwen-
Daghe*, or women's day of the old Dutch colo-
nists. She also records that first lake party to
Point Judith, given by her grandfather, Judge
Cooper, in August, 1799, but leaves the description of her father's lake parties to Mr. Keese:
"He was fond of picnic excursions on the lake,
generally to the *Three Mile Point*, and often
with a party of gentlemen to Gravelly, where
the main treat was a chowder, which their host
made up with great gusto. He could also brew a
bowl of punch for festive occasions, though he
himself rarely indulged beyond a glass of wine
for dinner." Concerning these festivities Mr.
Keese adds: "Lake excursions until 1840 were
made by a few private boats or the heavy, flat-
bottomed skiff which worthy Dick Case kept
moored at the foot of Fair Street. But Dick's

joints were too stiff to row more than an easy reach from the village; to the Fairy Spring was the usual measure of his strength. The Three Mile Point was the goal of the best oarsmen. Dick's successor in the thirties was an ugly horse-boat that in 1840 gave place to the famous scow of Joe Tom and his men, which for twenty years took picnic parties to the Point. A president of our country, several governors of the State, and Supreme Court judges were among these distinguished passengers. Doing such duty the scow is seen in the 1840 pictures of Cooperstown. No picnic of his day was complete without famous ' Joe Tom,' who had men to row the scow, clean the fish, stew potatoes, make coffee, and announce the meal. Rowing back in the gloaming of a summer's night, he would awake the echoes of Natty Bumppo's Cave for the pleasure of the company." At times a second echo would return from Hannah's Hill, and a third from Mt. Vision.

Between the lines can be read the hearty and cheery author's pleasure in all this merriment, yet, none the less, life's shadows exacted full attention, as the following shows: " Cooper took a generous and active part in sending relief to the starving people of Ireland; for, March 8, 1847, James Fenimore Cooper heads his town committee, and, 'in the name of charity and in obedience to the commands of God,' he urges

Joe Tom.

Natty's Cave.

[329]

an appeal 'from house to house, for *Food* is wanting that we possess in abundance.' "

" Cooper would admit of no denial of principle but could be lenient to offenders. One day he caught a man stealing fruit from his garden. Instead of flying into a passion, he told him how wrong it was to make the neighbors think there was no way of getting his fruit but by stealing it, and bid him the next time to come in at the gate and ask for it like a true man. Cooper then helped him to fill his basket and let him go." The author's fine fruit trees must have been tempting!

One day while walking in the garden with some ladies, Mr. Cooper led the way to a tree well laden with fine apples. Unable to reach them, he called to a boy in the street, and presenting him to his friends as one of the best boys in the village, — one who never disturbed his fruit, — he lifted the little fellow up to the branches to pick apples for the guests, and then filled his pockets as a reward for his honesty, and promised him more when he came again. The delighted boy waited for a few days and then repeated his visit to the tree, but forgetting to ask permission. Not knowing him from fre-

OTSEGO HALL — BACK VIEW.

quent intruders, Mr. Cooper's high voice from
a distance, added to the savage barking of his
watch-dog, frightened the well-meaning forager
into a resolve that he would not forget the
easier way next time of first asking before
picking.

The author's genuine interest in his home-
town folk never waned. Among the many and
sincere expressions of his good-will were the
free lectures he gave to the villagers. His

descriptions of naval actions were full of vigor.
On the blackboard he presented fleets, changing
their positions, moving ship after ship as the
contest went on, at the same time stating the
facts in history and using his cane as a pointer.

It is of note that Mr. Cooper's personal appearance in 1850 was remarkable. He seemed
in perfect health and highest energy and activity of faculties, but the autumn of this year
found him in New York City under mild ail-
ments. His friend, Mr. George Washington
Green, regretted not noting better his last talk
with the author about this time, of which he
says: "He excused himself that morning at
Putnam's for not rising to shake hands. ' My
feet,' said he, ' are so tender that I do not like
to stand longer than I can help.' Yet when we
walked together into Broadway, I could not help
turning now and then to admire his commanding figure and firm bearing. Sixty years seemed
to sit lightly on him. After a short stroll we
went to his room at the *Globe* and sat down to
talk. I never found him so free upon his own
works and literary habits. He confessed his
partiality for Leatherstocking. Said he: ' I
meant to have added one more scene and intro-

JAMES FENIMORE COOPER.
From a daguerreotype by Brady.

duced him in the Revolution, but I thought the public had had enough of him, and never ventured it.'"

Cooper's enjoyment of the marvelous voice of "The Swedish Nightingale," as Jenny Lind was called, the publication of his daughter's "Rural Hours," and the active progress of his own book sales are noted in his letter to his beloved wife.

BROADWAY HOTEL, Friday, Nov. 15, 1850.

MY DEAREST W., — Julia and Miss Thomas came down with me to hear Jenny Lind. " Have you heard

Jenny Lind?" "How do you like Jenny Lind?" are
the questions which supplant "Fine weather to-day"
and other similar comprehensive remarks. I am pa-
tiently waiting for the "Lake Gun" [a magazine ar-
ticle]. I am well and shall commence in earnest next

JENNY LIND AT CASTLE GARDEN, NEW YORK CITY, 1850.

week. Tell Sue [his daughter] I have seen Putnam,
who will be delighted to publish her new book. "Naval
History" is a little slack for the moment. There are
less than a hundred copies of second edition on hand
and the third must be shortly prepared. The fine edition will be published to-morrow. About two hundred
copies have been sent to the trade and with that issue
he will start. He has had five and twenty copies done
up in papier machia at $9.00. N—— is well. D. Z.

is still here. Old Peter is not yet married, but the affair is postponed until Spring, when the bride and groom will return to America. They wish to prolong the delightful delusion of courtship. I hope they may be as happy as we have been and love each other as much forty — days after their union as we do forty years. . . . . .

Yours

J. F. C.

At No. 1 Bond Street stood the old-time mansion of Dr. John W. Francis, where were welcomed many eminent in arts and letters at home and abroad, and where their host wrote his "Reminiscences of Sixty Years." Here it was that Cooper, on his last visit to New York, came seeking aid for his failing health. But with December the author returned to Cooperstown, whence he wrote a friend: " I have gone into dock with my old hulk, to be overhauled. Francis says I have congestion, and I must live low, deplete, and take pills. While I am frozen, my wife tells me my hands, feet, and body are absolutely warm. The treatment is doing good. You cannot imagine the old lady's delight at getting me under, in the way of food. I get no meat, or next to none, and no great matter in substitutes. This morning being Christmas, I

Dr. John W. Francis
and His Home
in New York City.

had a blow-out of oysters, and at dinner it will
go hard if I do not get a cut into the turkey.
I have lost pounds, yet I feel strong and clear-
headed. I have had a narrow escape, if I have
escaped."

The following spring Cooper again went to
New York City, whence he dates a letter to his
wife:

Saturday, March 29, 1851
COLLEGE HOTEL, NEW YORK

Your letter of Thursday has just reached me. I
am decidedly better. — Last night I was actually dis-
sipated. L. — came for me in a carriage and carried

me off almost by force to Doctor Bellows, where I met the Sketch Club, some forty people, many of whom I knew. I stayed until past ten, ate a water ice, talked a great deal, returned, went to bed fatigued and slept it off. — My friends are very attentive to me, they all seem glad to see me and think I am improving, as I certainly am. . . . I shall come home shortly. — I want to be in my garden and I wish to be in your dear hands, love, for though you know nothing you do a great deal that is right. Last evening I passed with Charlotte M. — who wanted to take me home to nurse me. There is no chance of seeing S.——.

Adieu, my love. . . . . . My blessing on the girls — all four of them.

J. F. C.

In April, 1851, the poet Bryant wrote of him: "Cooper is in town, in ill health. When I saw him last he was in high health and excellent spirits." These spirits were not dashed by the progressing malady that took him home to Cooperstown. Not realizing what illness meant, he bravely accepted what it brought, — the need to dictate the later parts of his "History of the United States Navy," and the "Towns of Manhattan," when he himself could no longer write. The latter was planned, partly written, and in press at the time of his death. That which was printed was burnt, the manuscript in part rescued, and finished by the pen of one of the family.

It was Fenimore Cooper's happiness to be blessed with a family whose greatest pleasure was to supply his every needed comfort; and one of his daughters was ever a companion in his pursuits, the wise and willing writer of his letters and dictations, and the most loving, never-tiring nurse of his latter days. Of these last months there is a pretty child-record by a friend who, " entering without notice," one day saw Mr. Cooper " lying at full length on the parlor floor, with a basket of cherries by his side. Upon his chest, vainly trying to bestride the portly form, sat his little grandson, to whom he passed cherries, and who, in turn, with childish glee, was dropping them, one by one, into his grandfather's mouth. The smiles that played over the features of child and man during this sweet and gentle dalliance were something not easily forgotten. A few months after this both child and man had passed beyond ' the smiling '; aye, and ' the weeping,' too."

Letters from Cooperstown led Dr. Francis to go there August 27, 1851, to see his esteemed friend in his own home. And of Cooper the

Doctor wrote: " I explained to him the nature of his malady — frankly assured him that within the limits of a week a change was indispensable to lessen our forebodings of its ungovernable nature. He listened with fixed attention. — Not a murmur escaped his lips. Never was information of so grave a cast received by any individual in a calmer spirit."

So passed the summer days of 1851 with the author, near his little lake, the Glimmerglass, and its Mt. Vision, when one mid-September Sunday afternoon, with his soul's high standard of right and truth undimmed, James Fenimore Cooper crossed the bar.

While from youth Cooper was a reverent follower of the Christian faith, his religious nature deepened with added years. Eternal truth grew in his heart and mind as he, in time, learned to look above and beyond this world's sorrows and failures. In July, 1851, he was confirmed in Christ's Church, — the little parish church just over the way from the old-Hall home, whose interests he had faithfully and generously served as sometime warden and as vestryman since 1834. Of one such service Mr. Keese writes that in 1840 the original

Christ's Church of Cooperstown underwent important alterations. Its entire interior was removed and replaced by native oak. As vestryman Mr. Cooper was prime mover and chairman of the committee of change, and hearing of the chancel screen in the old Johnstown church, first built by Sir William Johnson, he took a carpenter and went there to have drawings made of this white-painted pine screen, which at his own expense he had reproduced with fine, ornamental effect in oak, and made it a gift to Christ's Church. It was removed from Christ's Church about 1891, badly broken and abandoned. This

CHRIST'S CHURCH, COOPERSTOWN, N. Y.

so disturbed Cooper's daughters that his grandson, James Fenimore Cooper of Albany, New
York, had the pieces collected, and stored them
for using in his Cooperstown home; but he —
by request of the Reverend Mr. Birdsall — had

FENIMORE COOPER'S SCREEN GIFT.

them made into two screens for the aisles of the
church, where they were erected as a memorial to
his father, Paul Fenimore, and his great-grandfather, Judge William Cooper.   Mr. Keese's
words, dating January, 1910, are:

"And now comes in a rather singular discovery made by the writer a few days ago: In
looking over a book in my library, published

[342]

about ninety years ago, there is an article on Newstead Abbey, Nottinghamshire, England, with a steel engraving of the front of the Abbey, which is almost identical with the design of the original screen in Christ Church. Who was responsible for transplanting the same to this country appears to be unknown, but the fact is interesting in that Newstead Abbey was the home of the Byron family and that of Lord Byron."

In a letter of April 22, 1840, to H. Bleeker, Esq., Cooper wrote of this screen: " I have just been revolutionizing Christ's Church, Cooperstown, not turning out a vestry but converting its pine interior into oak — *bona fide* oak, and erecting a screen that I trust, though it may have no influence on my soul, will carry my name down to posterity. It is really a pretty thing — pure Gothic, and is the wonder of the country round."

Of Cooper himself was said: " Thus step by step his feet were guided into the ways of peace." It was of the Protestant Episcopal church that his wife's brother, William Heathcote de Lancey — a genius of goodness — was bishop.

A beautiful, tender, and touching tribute to the love of his life was Fenimore Cooper's will. In part it reads: " I, James Fenimore Cooper, give and bequeath to my wife, Susan Augusta,

BISHOP WILLIAM HEATHCOTE DE LANCEY.

all my property, whether personal or mixed, to be enjoyed by her and her heirs forever. I make my said wife the executrix of my will."

In a little over four months his wife followed him to the far country. Of his children, Elizabeth, the first-born, died in infancy; Susan Augusta, the author, was the second; the third, Caroline Martha, became Mrs. Henry Frederick Phinney; next came Anne Charlotte, then Maria Frances, who married Richard

Cooper; Fenimore, the first son, they lost in babyhood, and Paul Fenimore, the youngest, became a member of the bar in Albany, New York.

THE DE LANCEY ARMS.

Cooper left his family a competency, but the Hall home soon passed into other hands; later it was burnt. From rescued brick an attractive house was built on the west bank of the Susquehanna for his daughters Susan Augusta and Anne Charlotte, both now resting near father and mother in Christ's Church yard. Their niece, Miss Susan Augusta Cooper, daughter of their sister, Maria Frances, Mrs. Richard Cooper, now lives in this picturesque house, and there she reverently treasures many personal

The New Home and the Old Home.

belongings of her famous grandfather, and also those of her author-aunt, Susan Augusta Cooper, whose best memorial, however, is the noble orphanage on the river-bank some ways below. The oaken doors saved from the flames of the burning Hall served for this new

INDIAN HUNTER.

home, which overlooked the grounds of their old home. The site of the latter is marked by Ward's "Indian Hunter." Aptly placed, peering through mists of green toward the author's church-yard grave, he is a most fitting guardian of the one-time garden of Fenimore Cooper.

[347]

COOPER GROUNDS.

By the generosity of the late Mrs. Henry Codman Potter, this hunter's domain has been transformed into beautiful " Cooper Grounds " ; and here the red-man of bronze keeps ward and watch over memories that enshrine the genius of a noble soul whose records of this vanishing race are for all time.

A gentleman just from continental Europe in 1851 said of people there: " They are all reading Cooper." A traveler, returned from Italy about that time, wrote: " I found all they knew of America — and that was not a little — they had learned from Cooper's novels." When an eminent physician who was called to attend some German immigrants asked how they knew so much of their new-home country, they replied: " We learned it all from Cooper. We have four translations of his works in German, and we all read them." February 22, 1852, Charles G. Leland of Philadelphia wrote of Cooper's works: " There were several translations issued at Frankfort, Germany, in 1824, in two hundred and fifty parts, a second large edition in 1834, and a third in 1851. All his works, more than Scott and Shakespeare, are household words to the German people." Library records of to-day show no waning of this early popularity of the " Leatherstocking Tales " and " Sea Stories " of Fenimore Cooper. In 1883 Victor Hugo told General Wilson that excepting the authors of France, " Cooper was the greatest novelist of the century." It was Balzac who said: " If Cooper had succeeded in the painting of character to the same extent that he did in the painting the phenomena of nature, he would have uttered the last word of our art."

From Hanau-on-Main, Germany, January, 1912, Herr Rudolf Drescher writes: " Within two years two new translations of Cooper's complete works have been issued. One at Berlin, the other at Leipsic. 180 pictures by the artist Max Slevogt held one edition at $192, the other with less pictures was $60, and both were sold. Cheaper editions without pictures also met with large sales. I possess an 1826, German copy of ' The Pioneers.' " Another record is, Cooper's works have been seen " in thirty different countries, in the languages of Finland, Turkey and Persia, in Constantinople, in Egypt, at Jerusalem, at Ispahan."

The author's literary cruise, dating back three years before the launching of " The Pilot " in 1823, was a long one. And no admiral of mortal fame ever led so sturdy and motley a fleet — from the proud man-of-war to the light felucca, gondola, and bark-canoe — over ocean and inland waters. With visions of forests, its moving spirit and skilful pilot still stands at the helm, the full light of the ages upon " eye, arm, sail, spar, and flag." Thus is Fenimore Cooper firmly anchored in the mind and heart of posterity as the creator of American romance.

August, 1907, " Historic Cooperstown " held her Memorial Celebration. Her founder, Judge William Cooper, his hardy pioneers, and the " memory of one whose genius had given her Glimmerglass country world-wide fame," were honored with world-wide tributes. Among these were addresses, heartfelt, and able, from the late Bishop Henry Codman Potter, on " The Religious Future "; Francis Whiting Halsey, on " The Headwaters of the Susquehanna "; George Pomeroy Keese, on " Early Days of Cooperstown," and James Fenimore Cooper of Albany, New York, on his great-grandfather " William Cooper."

From "The Cooperstown Centennial" one learns that at five o'clock on Wednesday afternoon of August 7 many people were reverently taking part in solemn services around the grave of James Fenimore Cooper and beneath the glinting tree-shadows of Christ's Church yard. The service began with a procession of young girls in white surrounding the author's last resting-place, where verses on Cooper were recited by Miss Wilkinson; then the little folk sang the lyric tribute of Mr. Saxton:

> O, great magician, may the life
> We lead be such a one as thine —
> A simple life, transcending art,
> A spirit close to Nature's heart,
> A soul as strong and clear, and fine.

THE CHILDREN'S TRIBUTE.

After singing, the children, gathering around, covered the marble slab with their tributes — the flowers of the season. Some poetic pictures in blank verse were given of Cooper's works, by the Reverend Dr. W. W. Battershall of St. Peter's Church in Albany, New York, the present rector, and successor of Doctor Ellison, Cooper's boyhood instructor. Then the Rev. Ralph Birdsall, rector of the author's "little parish church," spoke of Fenimore Cooper's church-yard home: "A marble slab that bears no praise for fame or virtue; only a simple cross, symbol of the faith in which he lived and died, and upon which he based his hopes of immortality." The soldier lying near, brought from the field of honor; the author's old neighbors, who exchanged with him in life the friendly nod; hands that were calloused with the axe and shovel, and Judge Temple's aged slave in narrow home — all sleeping beneath the same sward and glancing shadows are not less honored now than is the plain, unpolished slab of stone, bearing two dates, — of birth and entrance into the life eternal of James Fenimore Cooper.

On his airy height of the "Cooper Memorial," gleaming white through the lakewood slope of

Mt. Vision, wondrous Leatherstocking stands, a rare tribute to simple, uplifting goodness. Clad in his hunting-shirt, deerskin cap, and leggings, his powder-horn and bullet-pouch swung over his shoulder, his dog Hector at his feet, looking up with speaking expression into the fine, wise, honest face of his master, stands Natty, gazing over all the lake he loved so well.

LAKE OTSEGO.

——o'er no sweeter lake
Shall morning break or noon-cloud sail;
No fairer face than thine shall take
The sunset's golden veil.

J. G. WHITTIER.

[354]

LEATHERSTOCKING.

" Cooper had no predecessor and no successor in his own field of fiction; he stood alone, — he was a creator, and his ' Natty ' will stand forever as the most original of pioneer characters," wrote Henry M. Alden.

With Rev. Mr. Birdsall, many think the time has come when the fame of Fenimore Cooper demands a world-given memorial in Cooperstown. A lifelike statue from an *artist's* chisel should show the " ' prose poet of the silent woods and stormy seas ' seated, pen in hand, gazing dreamily for inspiration over the Glimmerglass, where the phantom creatures of his genius brood." Let it stand, a new-world literary shrine, in the square fronting the old-Hall-

[355]

home site, which northward commands a sweeping view of his " little lake " and a side glimpse of lofty Leatherstocking of the tree-tops — not far away.

LEATHERSTOCKING MONUMENT.

And strewn the flowers of memory here.
For one whose fingers, years ago,
    Their work well finished, dropped the pen;
Whose master mind from land to sea
Drew forms heroic, long to be
    The living types of vanished men.

A. B. SAXTON.

In Memoriam

GEORGE POMEROY KEESE

O<small>N</small> April 22, 1910, and at the home of his son, Theodore Keese, in New York City, came the Spirit-Land call to the late George Pomeroy Keese. It was also in New York City that he was born, on January 14, 1828. His parents were Theodore Keese and Georgiann Pomeroy, niece of James Fenimore Cooper. This grand-nephew of the author enjoyed four score and more of full, active years, mostly spent in Cooperstown, N. Y., and he gave of them generously in serving the welfare and interests of that village. There Edgewater, Mr. Keese's attractive home, overlooks, from the south, the entire length and beauty of Lake Otsego, whose waters and banks are haunted by Cooper's creations.

From Mr. Keese is quoted:

"George Pomeroy of Northampton, Mass., came to Cooperstown among the early settlers in 1801. He married the only living sister of Fenimore Cooper in 1803.

"His ancestry dates back to the coming of William the Conqueror from Normandy in 1066.

At this time Ralph de Pomeroy accompanied the Norman duke to England and rendered him such valuable assistance that he received from him no fewer than fifty-eight lordships in Devonshire as a reward for his services. Selecting a favorable site, not far from the banks of the river Dart, Ralph de Pomeroy erected thereon the celebrated stronghold that now bears the family name of Berry-Pomeroy Castle, the stately ruins of which are still visited as one of the most picturesque objects of interest in the county of Devon.

" The descendants of the founder of Berry-Pomeroy retained the lands belonging to their ancestral home until the time of Edward VI, when at the period of the rebellion of that date they were seized by the crown and bestowed upon the haughty Lord Protector Somerset in whose family they still remain."

October 10, 1849, Mr. Keese married Caroline Adriance Foote, daughter of Surgeon Lyman Foote, U.S.A., who, with seven of their children, survives her husband. From childhood Mrs. Keese well knew Fenimore Cooper.

From his tender years to the age of twenty-four Mr. Keese lived in close touch with the author until his death in 1851. Afterwards such near association, affection and ability made Mr. Keese a veritable stronghold of authentic values concerning this grand-uncle. After his five years of patient, careful direction given to the preparation of this *personal* life of James Fenimore Cooper, the spirit of George Pomeroy Keese passed to the Land of Everlasting Light.

As a traveled, scholarly, wise, and gentle man, Mr. Keese kept in live pace with current events, and he possessed that strong, rare quality of character which " says little and does much," and compels esteem and devotion from all human kind.

Amongst Mr. Keese's various writings is " The Historic Records of Christ's Church, Cooperstown, N. Y." The rector, Reverend Ralph Birdsall, has written of its author: " At the altar of Christ's Church abides the secret that made Mr. Keese a man so widely honored and beloved."

MARY E. PHILLIPS.

RUINS OF BERRY-POMEROY CASTLE, 1825

INDEX

INDEX

Cooper, James, great-great-grandfather, 2.

Cooper, James Fenimore.
Accuracy, 106, 109, 115–118, 123, 127, 277, 282, 288–290; ancestry, 2–4; birth, 1; boyhood, 12, 13, 19, 23–35, 39; courage, 259, 273, 308; death, 340; honors, public, 99, 111–112, 114, 131, 192, 281; prices of works, 276–277, 350; industry, 43, 114; generosity, 57, 105–106, 219, 329, 332; screen gift, 340–343; love of art, 198, 203, 239–240; marriage, 68; name, change of, 2, 119–120; naval officer, 53–70; patriotism, 64, 79, 185, 232, 243, 258–260, 273; personality, 12, 49, 111–112, 149–152, 259, 267, 269, 280–281. Portraits: bust by d'Angers, 145; bust by Greenough, 198–200; daguerreotype by Brady, 279, 333; in oil by Jarvis, 91, 146; in oil by Madame de Mirbel, 143; Paris drawing (1827), 148; Yale silhouette, 39; sailor, the, 42–48; translations of works, 350.

Cooper, James Fenimore, grandson, x, 3–5, 342, 351.

Cooper, Maria Frances, daughter, 324, 342–345.

Cooper, Paul Fenimore, son, 100, 214, 216–217, 243, 342, 345.

Cooper, Richard Fenimore, brother, 20, 26, 62, 72.

Cooper, Richard Fenimore, nephew, 344, 345.

Cooper, Susan Augusta, wife, 63–65, 68, 71–72, 77, 98, 124–125, 132, 146–147, 154, 165–166, 247, 250, 264, 268, 314, 323–324, 334–338, 343–344.

Cooper, Susan Augusta, daughter, 13, 54, 71, 139, 142, 220, 243, 265, 268, 282, 314, 323–327, 334–335, 344–345, 347.

Cooper, Susan Augusta, granddaughter, 345, 347.

Cooper, William, father, 2, 4–11, 16, 34, 36, 42, 53, 62, 101, 103, 112, 342, 351.

Cooper, William, nephew, 142, 193.

Cooperstown, N. Y., xi, 15, 33, 69, 71, 274, 296–299, 315, 317, 328, 336, 338–348, 351–354.
Châlet Farm, 296–299, 311–314, 327.
"Chronicles of," 34, 102.
Fenimore Farm home, 71–72.
Manor, The, 8, 9, 103.
Otsego Hall, 8, 9, 16, 100, 261–265, 300, 317, 340, 345–347.
Otsego Lake, 4, 5, 6, 18–21, 27–28, 71, 104, 261, 265, 276, 282–286, 296, 324–328, 340, 356.
Three-Mile Point, 270–272, 327–328.

Cory, Master Oliver, 23–25.
"Crater, The," 308–309.
Croghan, Geo., xii.
Crosby, Enoch, 80, 86.

Dana, Richard Henry, 96, 111, 201.
"Deerslayer, The," 5, 282–286.
DeKay, James E., 93, 95.
Drake, Joseph Rodman, 92–93.
Drescher, Rudolf, 350.
Dunlap, William, 322–323.
Dwight, Timothy, 36, 37.

[366]

acement and damage.